ANCIENT
HISTORY

ANCIENT HISTORY

4 million years BC to AD 1066

CHANCELLOR
PRESS

This edition published by Chancellor Press
an imprint of Bounty Books
a division of Octopus Publishing Group Ltd.,
2-4 Heron Quays, London, England, E14 4JP

Printed in 2000

Produced by Miles Kelly Publishing Ltd.
Bardfield Centre, Great Bardfield, Essex, England
CM7 4SL

ISBN 0 75370 277 0

Produced by Toppan (HK) Ltd
Printed in China

Miles Kelly Publishing Limited

Publishing Director: Jim Miles
Editorial Director: Paula Borton
Art Director: Clare Sleven
Author: Brian Williams
Project Management: Neil de Cort
Editorial Assistant: Simon Nevill
Project Editor: Jane Walker
Designer: Jill Mumford
Artwork Commissioning: Natasha Smith, Kirsty Allen
and Suzanne Grant
Picture Research: Kate Miles and Janice Bracken
Lesley Cartlidge and Liberty Mella
Indexing: Lynn Bresler

The Publishers would like to thank the following
artists who have contributed to this book:

Rob Sheffield
Ross Watton (SGA)
Chris Forsey
Mike White (Temple Rogers)
Terry Riley Studio
Roger Gorringe (Illustration Ltd.)
Vanessa Card
Janos Marffy
Chris Odgers
Mike Foster (Maltings Partnership)

PHOTOGRAPHIC CREDITS
44 (BR) Robert Harding Picture Library; 57 (TR) Bernard and
Catherine Desjeux/CORBIS; 59 (TR) Graham King; 62 (BR)
Diego Lezanna/CORBIS; 72 (BR) Adam Woolfitt/CORBIS; 101
(CL) Werner Forman/CORBIS; 107 (TR) The Bridgeman Art
Library; 117 (BR) Robert Harding Picture Library.
All other images from the Miles Kelly Archive and Dover
Publications.

QUOTATION ACKNOWLEDGEMENTS
Extract from *The Rig Veda*, translated by Frederick Morgan,
published in *World Poetry* by W. W. Norton and Company; extract
from Homer: *The Iliad*, translated by Martin Hammond, published
by Penguin Classics; extract from Virgil: *The Aeneid*, translated by
W.F. Jackson Knight, published by Penguin; extract from
Herodotus: *The Histories*, translated by Aubrey De Sélincourt,
published Penguin; extract from Thucydides: *The History of the
Peleponnesian War*, translated by Rex Warner, published by Penguin;
extract from anonymous Han dynasty poem, translated by Dell R.
Hales, published in *World Poetry* by W. W. Norton and Company;
extract from Rumann: 'Storm at Sea', translated by Frank
O'Connor, published in *World Poetry* by W. W. Norton and
Company; extract from Justinian: 'Institutes', published in the
Oxford Dictionary of Quotations by the Oxford University Press;
extract from the *Popul Vuh*, translated by Dennis Tedlock, published
in *World Poetry* by W. W. Norton and Company; extract from
Murasaki Shikibu, her Diary and Poetic Memoirs, translated by Richard
Bowring, published by Princeton University Press; all extracts
from the works of St. Augustine published in the Oxford
Dictionary of Quotations by the Oxford University Press; extract
from Venerable Bede: *Ecclesiastical History of the English Nation*,
published in Internet Medieval Sourcebook, Fordham University
Centre for Medieval Studies; extract from Alfred the Great: *Whole
Works*, published by Jubilee Edition; 'On the Viking Raids',
translated by Frank O'Connor, published in *World Poetry* by W. W.
Norton and Company.

Contents

How to use this book 8

Introduction 10

What is History? 12

Work of Archaeologists 14

Work of Historians 16

The First Humans 18

The First People 20

The Great Migrations 22

The Ice Age 24

The First Farmers 26

The First Civilizations 28

Mesopotamia and Sumer 30

Society and Government 32

Cities and Temples 34

Babylon 36

Indus Valley 38

Crete and Mycenae 40

Megalithic Europe 42

Egypt 44

Pyramids and Gods 46

The Jews 48

Phoenicians and Assyrians 50

China 52

War and Weapons 54

African Empires 56

Olmecs and Chavin 58

Empires East and West 60

Persian Empire 62

Rise of Greece 64

Greek Literature and Art 66

Trade and Colonies 68

Alexander the Great 70

Aryan India 72

Eastern religions 74

China 76

Japan 78

Celtic Europe 80

Rise of Rome 82

Roman Empire 84

War and government 86

Greek and Roman religion 88

The Early Middle Ages 90

Byzantine Empire 92

The Maya and Teotihuacan 94

Rise of Islam 96

Fujiwara Japan 98

China Tang dynsasty 100

Muslim empires 102

Religion and monasticism 104

Anglo-Saxons, Picts, Welsh
and Irish 106

Franks and Charlemagne 108

Alfred the Great 110

The Vikings 112

Trade and towns 114

The Norman Conquest 116

Timeline and reference section 118
Index 123

The quickest way to find out about a period of history that interests you is to look at the Contents list on page 6. If you do not see a heading that is the same as the subject you are searching for, look in the Index (pages 123–128). It will help you to find the information you want.

How to Use This Book

As well as chapters on subjects such as ancient Egypt or Alexander the Great, there are also special feature chapters which look at developments during a certain period, and feature examples from more than one country.

These feature chapters cover topics such as society and government, religions, war and weapons, and trade and towns. From them you can discover how people did things and how human lives changed over time. You will also learn how life in the ancient world was in some ways not so different from our own way of life today.

Each chapter in the book contains a timeline with key dates for the period. To find the birth and death dates of a famous person, or when a certain ruler was in power, look in the timeline in the chapter in question or turn to the reference section which starts on page 118. It contains a great deal of information about the people and places of the ancient world.

Dates

Every ancient civilization had its own calendar. Today there are several religious calendars in use, for example the Jewish and the Islamic calendars. For practical convenience, most of the world uses the Christian calendar, which begins with the birth of Jesus Christ. Much of the history in this book took place before that date.

In most books, the letters BC and AD are used with dates. The letters BC after a date indicate the number of years before the birth of Jesus Christ (which for this purpose is taken to be the non-existent year 0). The letters AD (which stand for the Latin *Anno Domini*, meaning 'in the year of Our Lord') are used with dates after Christ's birth. The letters BC and AD are used throughout this Encyclopedia.

This is a quick-reference guide to the time span covered by the double page.

The timeline provides you with the important dates from the period.

This panel will appear on some pages. It will give you the views and comments of someone writing at the time.

War and Weapons

War has been a part of life for as long as humans have existed. Prehistoric people fought for territory and food, using rocks and sticks as weapons. Later, they used stone-tipped spears and bows and arrows.

The discovery of bronze in about 3500 BC brought the first revolution in weaponry. Bronze swords and spear points were sharper than stone and bone weapons. Iron was even stronger still. Peoples of the Near East, such as the Hittites, were the first to master iron-making.

Armies and armour

Each of the ancient Near East superpowers rounded up civilians to serve in armies for the conquest of other countries, and for defence against enemies. To protect themselves, soldiers began wearing armour on their

▷ *Assyrian troops used wheeled siege towers with iron-tipped rams to batter down the walls of enemy towns.*

Timeline:

A sculpture shows an Egyptian king pictured defeating an enemy.	3100 BC
Sumerians make bronze war axes and spear points.	2500 BC
Body armour used by Egyptians and Mesopotamians.	2000 BC
Chariots in use in Egypt and Near East. Sickle-shaped swords of bronze.	1500 BC
First iron swords. End of Trojan War.	1200 BC
Assyrian armies include infantry, cavalry and chariots.	800 BC

△ *Egyptian soldiers fought with spears, axes, clubs, javelins (throwing spears) swords and bows and arrows. Trumpeters blew signal calls to direct the troops in the confusion of battle.*

bodies. By the time of the Trojan War, about 1200 BC, armour was made from metal plates fastened with leather thongs. Soldiers wore metal helmets to protect the head, and carried shields (usually round or rectangular). Some warriors scorned armour – the Greeks and Celts sometimes fought practically naked.

The first organized armies

Kings had small bodyguards of trained soldiers, including chariot-drivers, but they still relied on untrained peasants as foot soldiers. The Assyrians organized the first 'professional' army, and were greatly feared because of its ferocity. An Assyrian army included cavalry (soldiers on horses) and infantry (soldiers on foot).

Assyrian soldiers wore chainmail armour, and fought with iron swords and spears. Archers rode into battle on chariots, then sheltered behind basketwork shields to fire and reload. Slingers hurled stones, often farther than a javelin.

Infantry and cavalry

In China, soldiers traditionally fought on foot, and in huge armies (as many as 100,000 men). Facing marauders on horseback, the Chinese had to become horse-soldiers too. The Chinese composite bow of wood and bone had a longer range than a simple bow. Chinese archers also used crossbows.

Hittite charioteers

The Hittites, a fierce people from Anatolia (modern Turkey), were the first to use chariots in war. Hittite archers fired their arrows from these chariots, giving them a great advantage.

△ *Axe heads were made from bronze (shown here) and iron. A popular weapon, particularly among Chinese troops, was a halberd, a long spear with an axelike head. It was used for fighting at close quarters.*

> There was the clash of shields, of spears and the fury of men cased in bronze... Then there were mingled the groaning and the crowing of men killed and killing.
>
> THE ILIAD, HOMER (8TH CENTURY BC)

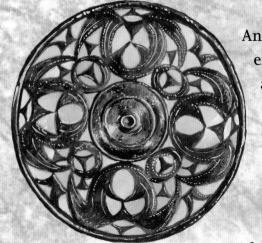

Ancient History is designed to be easy to use while you enjoy its information-packed pages. The book is arranged in four main sections, each covering a period of time with a particular theme.

Introduction

Within each section are a number of two-page chapters. Each of these chapters deals with a specific aspect of history. This could be an important region or period, or a famous person or culture. It could also give you some extra information on a subject, like the first towns, or the development of weapons.

The opening section is called The First Humans and deals with the origins of humankind from its beginnings in Africa. It explains the evolution of humans from our

▽ The old mosque at Mecca. The Islamic prophet Muhammad used to pray outside in his courtyard, and his followers still pray outside today.

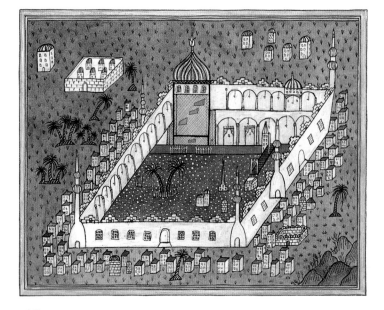

10

△ Arab trading ships were famous for their long voyages. They travelled across the Indian Ocean to Indonesia, and then even further afield to China.

▽ After they had conquered England, the Normans built castles across the country to protect their new lands.

ancestors, the apes. It covers the Stone Age and the last Ice Age, and ends with the beginning of organized farming. Other sections cover The First Civilizations, Empires East and West and The Early Middle Ages.

Ancient History covers a very long span of human prehistory as well as ancient history. It begins with the first humans, who lived more than one million years ago. The book ends in the last century of the first millennium (the AD 1000s), with the close of the early Middle Ages.

▷ This is called the 'Alfred jewel'. It is believed to have belonged to King Alfred the Great.

We live in a world of rapid changes, and to many people anything that happened more than 10 years ago is history! Of course it is, and some historians spend their time studying the events of the past 10, 50 or 100 years.

What is History?

Many historians consider the beginning of the 'modern world' to be in the 1400s – with the Renaissance in Europe. This was a time of new ideas and exploration, but it was also a time when people rediscovered the ancient past. The ancient world helped to shape the new world.

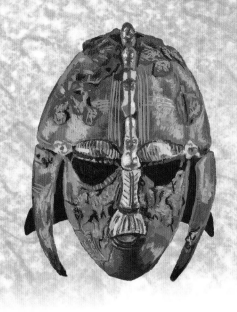

△ This iron helmet was part of a series of treasures and artefacts unearthed at a burial site called Sutton Hoo.

▽ William the Conqueror invaded England in AD 1066. He was the first of the Norman kings.

A long line of civilizations

Human history stretches back far beyond the invention of writing, about 5,000 years ago, reaching back even before the first farmers planted crops. For most of this time, Europe and America played little part in changing the world. Africa and Asia produced the first towns, the first farms, new wealth and new ideas.

Our modern technological civilization is the latest in a long series of civilizations. It is more widespread than any other, but still young – it has been around for fewer than 500 years. The civilizations you can read about in this book were smaller than our own, but some were much, much older. The civilization of ancient Egypt lasted 3,000 years. Chinese civilization was more or less unbroken for just as long, up until the 20th century.

Modern world, ancient traditions

The modern world has grown out of these ancient civilizations. Ancient peoples gave us the wheel, pottery, writing, mathematics, music, painting and sculpture. They measured the Earth and studied the stars. The temples of the Maya in Central America are in ruins today, but local people still speak Mayan languages and follow ancient traditions. The Pyramids, the Parthenon and the Great Wall of China still make visitors stand and stare in awe. The empires of the past have left their mark on the present.

Of course, history does not begin and end in neat sections. It is a flow of events and people, merging and overlapping with each other. One civilization influences another. People borrow from their neighbours. Wars of conquest reshape people's lives and customs. One empire falls, and another rises in its place.

△ The Hippodrome. This was a giant arena where the Byzantine emperors held chariot races and gladiatorial contests to entertain the people.

Links to the past

Western art and philosophy, and our ideas of government, owe much to the Greeks and Romans, who in turn took many ideas from the civilizations of Persia, Babylon and Egypt. The ancient world gave us the great religions of Hinduism, Buddhism, Judaism, Christianity and Islam. It gave us our languages. Its myths and legends were handed down from generation to generation, to become part of our folklore. In so many ways, we are linked to our ancient past, and to the people who lived there. They were our ancestors after all, human beings just like us.

△ Astronomy flourished as a science in the Islamic world. The Arab astronomers were among the first to name some of the brightest stars.

▷ Trajan's column. This is a part of a giant monument that the Roman emperor Trajan built to record his deeds. It also shows the day-to-day tasks of the Roman army.

The word 'archaeology' comes from two Greek words and means 'the study of old things'. It is now a science, which uses techniques that make it possible for us to find out about people who lived long ago, long before history was written.

Archaeology

Many archaeological discoveries are made by digging in the ground at sites where ancient people lived. A city is often built in layers. The shops and offices of today stand on the ruins of temples and markets from the past. So a building site in a city may reveal unexpected finds. A low tide may uncover a ring of sacred wooden posts, built thousands of years ago and later covered by the sea and shifting sand.

▽ *Medieval monks spent some of their time copying out illuminated (decorated) books, mostly of religious texts.*

Planning and recording

Archaeologists work methodically and carefully. Photographs taken from the air may reveal outlines of a road or building that are invisible on the ground. A device called a magnetometer can detect pottery kilns or iron-working hearths. Metal detectors occasionally turn up buried treasures, such as hoards of old coins, jewellery or weapons.

When archaeologists start to explore a site, they mark it out in a grid pattern to make an accurate plan, on which the location of each find is recorded. Wood and cloth rot, but traces of them may survive even after hundreds, or thousands, of years. Pottery, glass and metal last longer. Each piece found is cleaned and numbered.

A rubbish pit can tell experts what people ate, because animal bones, shells and seeds are often preserved in it. Graves may contain 'grave goods' buried with the dead person, such as weapons, jewellery and pottery. A skeleton can reveal medical evidence of how a person died and how healthy he or she was in life.

How old?

During the 19th century a Danish archaeologist, Christian Jurgensen Thomsen, suggested that there were three 'ages' of ancient history. He called them the Stone Age (the oldest), the Bronze Age and the Iron Age – after

△ Frankish (French) soldiers heading for battle under the command of King Charlemagne in the late AD 700s.

▽ Hadrian's wall. This border, which is 118km long, was built by the Romans in AD 122 to defend their northern frontier against invasion.

the kinds of tools people used in each period. We still use these names, but it is important to remember that the ages happened at different times in different places.

Two useful scientific methods of dating objects are radiocarbon dating (used for wood, charcoal and bones) and thermoluminescence (used for burned stones and pottery).

Famous finds

Archaeological work was first carried out seriously in the 1800s, when some of the most famous finds were made. The Rosetta Stone, found in AD 1822 by the French in Egypt, contains the same words in three forms of ancient writing: hieroglyphics, a simpler form of Egyptian script and Greek. Scholars could read the Greek and the simple Egyptian writing, so they were able to decode the hieroglyphics and read the many ancient inscriptions that had previously baffled them.

The German archaeologist Heinrich Schliemann discovered the site of Troy in the AD 1870s. Probably the most sensational find of the 20th century came in AD 1922, when British archaeologist Howard Carter dug into the undisturbed tomb of the pharaoh Tutankhamun.

More important 20th-century discoveries about the ancient world came when Sir Leonard Woolley found the graves of the kings of Sumer at Ur, and when Sir Arthur Evans found the ruins of the Minoan palace of Knossos on the island of Crete. There have been many other fascinating finds – the uncovering of the Roman town of Pompeii buried by a volcanic eruption in AD 79, the excavation in AD 1939 of the 7th-century Sutton Hoo ship in England and the discovery of the tomb of the Chinese emperor Shih Huang-di, with its army of terracotta soldiers, in AD 1974. Each new discovery tells us more about the ancient world. As archaeology develops further, new finds will continue to be made.

History comes from a Greek word meaning 'what is known by asking'. The job of a historian is to ask questions and make sense of the answers.

Historians

The Greeks were among the first people to write history based on first-hand 'reporting' of the facts. Herodotus (who died in 425 BC) wrote about the wars between the Greeks and the Persians. He travelled and talked to people who had taken part in the wars. Another Greek historian was Thucydides, who wrote a history of the Peloponnesian War between Athens and Sparta. He took part in the fighting and met war leaders.

Stories and legends

Historians work from a viewpoint. The first people to write their own history were the Chinese. We know the name of one early Chinese historian, Sima Qian, who wrote a history of China in about 100 BC. The Egyptians and other peoples recorded the names of their kings, as well as victories in battles.

Early historians were keen to show their own side in a good light. People felt it was important to write down the stories and legends about the past, and show how their state had come into existence. The Roman historian Livy collected scraps of information from various sources, listened to stories passed down by word of mouth, and turned them into the first full history of the Romans (up to the year 9 BC). Another Roman writer, Tacitus, wrote of the period from AD 14 to 96. He wrote about the Roman wars with the Celts in Germany and Britain. Since the Celts left no written histories of their own, we have only his description of what they were like, and of what happened. Sometimes people who made history also wrote it. Julius Caesar, the Roman general, wrote his own book about his campaigns in Gaul.

Ordinary lives

Before the AD 1900s, historians were mostly interested in governments and famous people. Today, historians are just as interested in the lives of ordinary men and women – how they lived, what they ate, the clothes they wore, the work they did, and so on. Some historians are interested in how economic changes affect people. Others study military history (wars and weapons), the history of the arts or the development of religion.

▽ *These beautiful illuminations were produced by monks. It was very time-consuming, but the monks felt that this showed their dedication to God.*

▷ The Frankish King Charlemagne introduced this writing, called 'Carolingian script', which was easier for people to read and write.

▽ During the Stone Age people used scrapers to clean the hides of hunted animals.

What kind of source?

Like a detective, the historian relies on evidence. It may include writings such as books, law documents, letters, wills and even household bills. Many different kinds of sources may contain clues.

Historians have primary and secondary sources. Primary sources are documents or objects made in the period being studied, for example a stone marked with Egyptian hieroglyphs or a mummy. Secondary sources are materials prepared later by people who saw the primary sources. A Roman traveller's account of his visit to Egypt is a secondary source, so is a drawing made in the 1700s of a tomb or monument which was later damaged or altered. To study the ancient world, where written records often do not exist, historians rely on evidence found by archaeologists.

△ A Mayan priest.

The beginning of human history can be traced back long before the first human beings appeared – to the earliest forms of life on Earth about 3,000 million years ago. Of the enormous variety of animals that evolved over millions of years, among the most advanced were tree-living mammals called primates. These included the first apes.

The First Humans

About 10 million years ago, some apes left the trees to walk on the open plains. They had large brains, and used their fingers to pick up food. About 4 million years ago, the humanlike ape *Australopithecus* (southern ape) lived in Africa. It probably used sticks or stones as tools, in the same way that chimpanzees do.

The first humans
The first human species was *Homo habilis* (handy man), who lived in East Africa 2 million years ago. By 1.5 million years ago, the more advanced *Homo erectus*

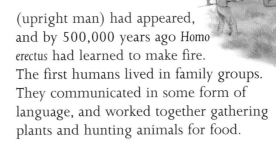

(upright man) had appeared, and by 500,000 years ago *Homo erectus* had learned to make fire. The first humans lived in family groups. They communicated in some form of language, and worked together gathering plants and hunting animals for food.

Modern humans

About 400,000 years ago, a new species, more like us and known to scientists as *Homo sapiens* (wise man), had become the dominant human species. These humans made tools from stone and other materials. This 'stone age' lasted until about 10,000 years ago, although isolated groups of people carried on using stone tools until the present day.

In a series of migrations, humans spread to every continent. They crossed over land bridges, which were uncovered as sea water turned to ice during the Ice Age. People moved in groups from Africa across Europe and Asia, and into America and Australasia. Their social organization and developing technology helped them to survive the harsh climate of the Ice Age.

Hunters become farmers

About 10,000 years ago, people became farmers for the first time. They planted crops, and kept goats, cattle and sheep. The earliest centres of the farming revolution were in the Near East and Asia. Here, people first settled in towns and developed a new way of life – the beginnings of civilization.

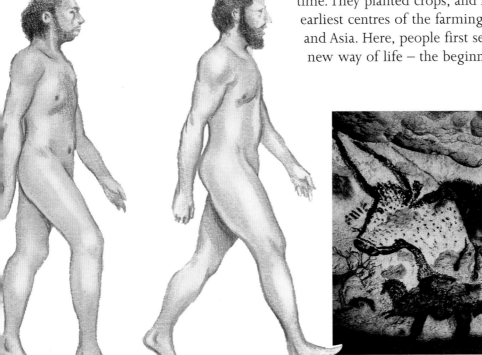

BC

400,000 BC
100,000 BC
20,000 BC
10,000 BC
4,000 BC
2,000 BC

The first modern human was *Homo sapiens* (meaning 'wise man'), who appeared between 400,000 and 300,000 years ago. His body looked like ours, but he had a large brain and small jaws. His limbs were longer and straighter than those of earlier people.

The First People

The ape-humans had used tools that were simply pebbles picked up from the ground. *Homo sapiens* were much more skilful, choosing stones with care. They chipped or flaked off bits to make shaped tools including hand axes, choppers, knives and scrapers. These people also made use of other materials, such as animal bones and horns. The new humans spread from Africa into new territories. Several early forms of *Homo sapiens* seem to have lived in Africa, the Near East and Asia. By about 35,000 years ago they had reached Europe and Australia.

Early modern human (Homo sapiens) appears.	*c.* 350,000 BC
Neanderthal people appear.	*c.* 120,000 BC
Modern human (Homo sapiens sapiens) appears.	*c.* 100,000 BC
Modern humans spread to Europe and later to Australia.	*c.* 40,000 BC
Cro-Magnons appear in Europe	*c.* 33,000 BC
Neanderthals either die out or are interbred into modern human populations.	*c.* 30,000 BC
Hunters roam Europe. Cave paintings are made.	*c.* 13,000 BC
Latest date for people to reach America from Asia.	*c.* 11,000 BC

Neanderthals

In Europe there was another human species, known as Neanderthal man, who for a time lived alongside modern humans. Scientists think Neanderthals were a 'side branch' of *Homo sapiens*, who had adapted for life in the cold climates of the last Ice Age.

Neanderthal people lived in Europe from about 100,000 to 35,000 years ago. They sheltered in caves, made fire and hunted animals using stone tools and wooden spears.

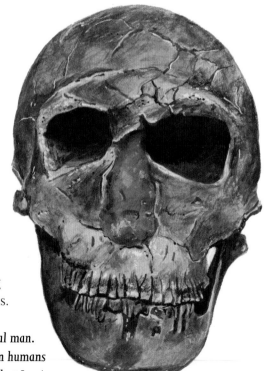

▷ The large skull of a Neanderthal man. These people lived alongside modern humans during the last Ice Age.

20

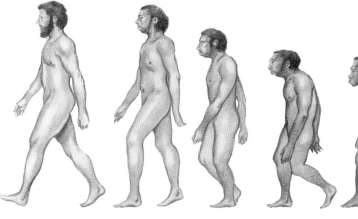

 Early peoples gradually looked less like humanoid apes and more like human beings. Their bodies became more suited to walking upright, and legs became longer than arms.

| Modern man | Neanderthal man | Upright man | Handy man | Southern ape |

△ Stone Age people hunted with bows, spears and flint axes. On the American grasslands, groups of hunters drove to extinction large grazing animals such as mastodons and giant bison.

Although they had large brains, the heavily built Neanderthals were slower moving and less adaptable than the newcomers who started moving into Europe about 40,000 years ago. The Neanderthals were either wiped out by competition from other groups, or integrated into humanity through interbreeding.

Cro-Magnons

The newcomers in Europe were the Cro-Magnons, who are named after the site in France where a group of their skeletons was discovered in 1868. Their bone structure was very similar to ours today. Cro-Magnons were probably our direct ancestors. Neanderthals and modern humans may have lived side by side, and even bred between themselves. Yet it was the Cro-Magnons who won the evolutionary race.

The Stone Age

Historians call this period of prehistory the Stone Age, because stone was the most important material used by the first tool-makers. These early stone-crafting techniques show surprising skill.

Neanderthal burial

Neanderthals were the first humans to bury the dead. Archaeologists have found evidence of Neanderthal burial ceremonies. The remains of tools and meat have been found in graves, showing that the dead were buried with care.

Hand axe

Scraper

Spear head

△ Stone Age tools. Both the hand axe and scraper were made from flint. Spear heads were shaped from deer antlers. The hand axe was probably the most important early Stone Age tool.

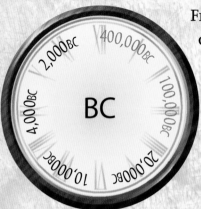

From Africa, humans began to spread to every continent – a process which took almost one million years. Everywhere, humans were on the move. This was the age of the great migrations.

The Great Migrations

The Neanderthals vanished from Europe, although small groups may have remained in remote places. Modern humans moved across Europe and Asia, and started to explore America and Australia. A wetter climate over the whole world produced a green region of lakes and grasslands in what is now the Sahara Desert. Animals and people thrived in these surroundings.

Cro-Magnons move into Europe from the Near East. — *c.* 38,000 BC

People reach America and Australia from Asia. — *c.* 33,000 BC

Neanderthals die out. — *c.* 28,000 BC

Evidence of cave people in Brazil. — *c.* 23,000 BC

Last wet period in Saharan North Africa. — *c.* 13,000 BC

People reach the tip of South America. — *c.* 8000 BC

British Isles cut off by rising sea levels. — *c.* 3000 BC

People reach Pacific Islands by boat. — *c.* 2000 BC

Nomads, or wanderers, moved constantly to find fresh food supplies. Small groups of people walked across continents, following the animals that they hunted for food.

Some moved into the north of Asia and even travelled across to what is now Alaska (in North America), but most of these early peoples on the move headed towards warmer regions. They began to settle on grassy plains and close to water. Everyone lived in close harmony with nature, and their lives were regulated by the seasons.

We can form an idea of what early human life was like from studies of the Australian Aborigines. Until the 18th century, these people had little contact with the world beyond Australia. A few isolated

△ *Aboriginal rock artists looked "beneath the skin" to show a person's bones or organs. Paintings of people and animals are found at sites linked in Aboriginal belief to the Dream Time, when spirits created the world.*

Making fires

People made fire using a simple wooden stick called a fire drill. The drill was turned quickly over a piece of dry wood until it produced enough heat to start the fire.

groups of people in parts of South America and Southeast Asia also preserved a 'Stone Age' way of life into the modern age.

The Aborigines

The Aborigines probably reached Australia overland, crossing a land bridge that joined New Guinea to Australia 30,000 years ago. They had boats, so sea migrations were also possible. There is even a theory that some crossed the Pacific Ocean and landed in America.

Food, clothes and tools

These people lived by food gathering and hunting. Along the coast, they fished with nets, basket traps and spears. In the bush, they used fire to drive animals into traps, and made poisons from leaves and roots to drug fish in pools. Women and children collected roots, fruits, insects and honey from wild bees' nests. They wore no clothes and rubbed animal fats onto their bodies to protect themselves from cold.

Technology was simple. The Aborigines made simple stick shelters. They made stone tools and knew how to use bows and arrows as well as spear-throwers. The boomerang was used for hunting and war.

Paintings and dances

On rocks and cave walls, artists used coloured earth to make paintings, telling stories of myths and legends. This rock art, and the songs and dances of the people, reveal spiritual beliefs. One of the most powerful beliefs was the notion of the 'Dream Time' – this was the time when all living things were created.

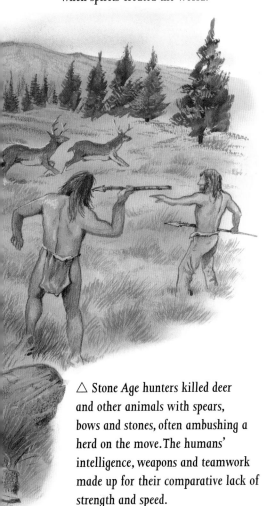

△ *Stone Age hunters killed deer and other animals with spears, bows and stones, often ambushing a herd on the move. The humans' intelligence, weapons and teamwork made up for their comparative lack of strength and speed.*

△ *The Aborigines used ritual boomerangs, decorated with secret symbols, in magical dances.*

BC

2,000 BC 400,000 BC 100,000 BC 20,000 BC 10,000 BC 4,000 BC

Around 18,000 years ago, the last of a series of Ice Ages gripped much of the Northern Hemisphere. Icecaps spread southwards across Europe and North America. The sea level fell, uncovering land bridges which animals and people crossed – between Asia and Alaska for example.

The Last Ice Age

This last Ice Age had a dramatic effect on people's way of life. The spread of snow and ice reduced the size of the areas in which they could live. Many moved away to seek warmer regions. Other groups adapted to living in the freezing conditions. Clothed only in animal skins, and sheltering in caves and tents, people tried to survive around the fringes of the vast ice sheets.

Hunters make clay figures of people and animals. — c. 23,000 BC

Cave made paintings about this time at Lascaux in France and Altamira in Spain. — c. 23,000 BC

Last Ice Age reaches its coldest point. Earliest rock art known in Asia. — c. 16,000 BC

Tool-making

People who kept themselves alive by hunting needed good weapons and tools. They made these from flints, choosing stones that were easily chipped or flaked to create useful cutting and scraping edges. Where good flints were found, people dug mines to hack out the stones. They set up tool-making 'factories' where they made polished stone axes and other tools with great skill.

Hunter-gatherers cross from Asia into North America via the exposed Bering Strait. — c. 14,000 BC

End of the last Ice Age. Possible first domestic animal - the dog - used for hunting. — c. 11,000 BC

New Stone Age begins. — c. 6,000 BC

▷*As well as being an important source of meat, woolly mammoths provided skins for clothing and shelter. Their bones and tusks were carved into tools and decorative ornaments.*

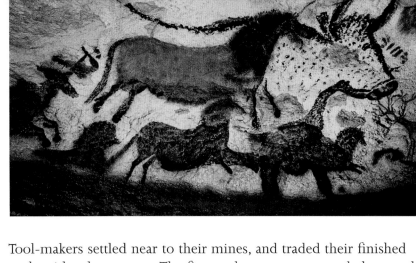

▷ Cave artists used natural paints made from coloured earth and plant juices. Their drawings may have been made for ritual magic, to bring success to a group's hunters.

△ This Ice Age man is using a stone blade to scrape clean the skin of a hunted animal.

Tool-makers settled near to their mines, and traded their finished tools with other groups. The first trade routes were made by people travelling from one place to another to exchange goods. In boggy areas, the first 'roads' were made – consisting of wooden walkways built from logs. Near rivers and lakes, people became skilled boatmen and fishermen, making their craft from hollowed-out tree trunks and bundles of reeds. They wove fishing nets, and built lakeside huts on stilts. They made fire with friction (rubbing) techniques, using a bowdrill or striking flints. Once a fire was lit, people did their best to make sure it did not go out.

Social life

People living in groups had to find ways of working together. They developed ideas of sharing tasks between men and women, and between individuals. Expert tool-makers (perhaps women or the elderly) stayed in camp while others went hunting – and so had more time to practise their skills for the benefit of the group.

By working together, early humans were able to hunt and kill big animals such as mammoth and bison.

Hut of mammoth bones

Ice Age hunters made shelters from the bones of mammoths. They made the framework of bones and filled in the gaps with skins, turf and moss. Groups of men drove the animals into swamps, where they became trapped and were killed with spears or rocks.

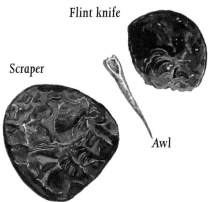

Flint knife

Scraper

Awl

△ Tools for scraping were made mostly from flint. This hard material could be chipped into tools of many different shapes and sizes. Other tools were made from bone, antlers and tusks.

BC

About 10,000 years ago the icecap had shrunk. Warmer weather made life much easier and human groups began to grow. In places, people who used to wander around looking for food found that by gathering wild cereal plants such as rice and wheat, and sowing the seeds, they could grow new plants in the same place.

The First Farmers

People naturally chose plants with the largest grain-heads. A chance cross-breeding of wheat and wild grass in the Jordan Valley in Israel produced a new wheat with bigger grains. People found that grinding the grains gave flour to make bread, an important new food. How this breakthrough in skill and diet happened is not clear, but it changed history.

Sheep may have been domesticated.	c. 9000 BC
Start of farming in the Near East. Walls of Jericho, the earliest town, built.	c. 8000 BC
Wheat and barley are grown in the Near East. Pigs and cattle are domesticated.	c. 7000 BC
Farming spreads west into Europe and east into Asia. Copper in use. Pottery made.	c. 6000 BC
First use of brick for building in the Near East.	c. 5000 BC
First farmers cross to Britain. First ploughs used in Near East.	c. 4000 BC
Invention of the wheel in Mesopotamia. Use of copper tools spreads.	c. 3500 BC
Domestication of the horse in central Asia.	c. 2500 BC

Settling down

People no longer wandered after herds of wild animals or in search of fresh plants to pick. Instead, some stayed in one place, making homes beside their new plots of roughly tilled and sown ground. They had become farmers.

Rivers and lakes were good places to settle. Fish could be caught in nets, and water channelled along ditches to the new fields. The first farmers made new tools, such as wooden digging sticks and sickles with flint blades, to harvest their crops. Farmers tamed animals too. Hunters had already tamed wolf cubs to help in the hunt, but now domestic dogs were trained to herd flocks of sheep and goats. Farm animals were bred

Dogs and poultry

Populations grew after the Ice Age. People could not find enough food by the old way of hunting and gathering. A new strategy was needed to survive; farming and the raising of domestic animals.

△ Early tools were made from materials such as flint, bone and antlers. Common ones were the flint sickle (right), the flint and wood hammer (centre) and the antler pick (left).

from young wild animals, captured and raised among people. Domesticated animals were then bred to make them more docile and suitable for human use.

Farmers and new tools

The first farmers lived in the Near East, across a region stretching west from the Nile Valley to the Tigris and Euphrates rivers. This area became known as the Fertile Crescent. Farming also developed in other continents at this time – in China and in the Americas.

With farming came new inventions and skills. People made pottery and invented the wheel, used first of all to turn the clay as it was shaped. They made metal tools, first from cold-beaten copper (about 8,500 years ago), then from bronze (a mixture of copper and tin formed by heat). About 5,000 years ago, people learned how to smelt (melt and separate) iron ore from rocks. They used the iron to make tools, both for peace and war.

Iron Age world

Farming brought new wealth. Trade grew and so did warfare. The richer people clustered together to defend themselves against raids by envious enemies. Village life demanded a communal form of government. Chieftains who had once led bands of nomads became rulers of villages. Some of the villages grew rapidly into the world's first towns. Civilization had begun.

◁ The first farmers made their own homes, clothes and tools. In a good year, their crops gave them more food than they needed, so they traded this surplus with neighbours. They also had domestic animals.

△ The first farmers began to develop new skills, which included the use of fire to make metal tools and weapons. The tools seen here are (from left to right): a sickle for harvesting crops, a knife, and a pair of pincers.

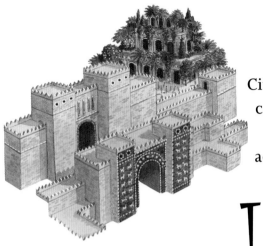

Civilization began with the first towns. Towns grew into cities, which became the centres of the world's first empires. Egypt, the Indus Valley and China all had advanced societies.

The First Civilizations

Impressive civilizations also arose in central America, Africa south of the Sahara and the eastern Mediterranean. Religion, trade, art and law-making developed. So did technology – and warfare. Human life became more organized and complex.

The first towns

The oldest known town ruins are those of Jericho – its walls date from about 11,000 years ago. The ruins of Catal Huyuk, in Turkey, date from about 8,250 years ago. People built towns in Mesopotamia, Egypt, the Indus Valley, China and Central America. Rivers were the cradles of these new civilizations, attracting farmers and traders. Towns became marketplaces, and cities became centres of government.

Kings and cities

The early city-states were led by kings, who made laws. Often kings were also priests. Powerful kings such as Sargon of Akkad

and Hammurabi of Babylon ruled the first empires. The pharaohs of Egypt lived in imperial splendour, in a land made rich by farming and trade. Other rulers built luxurious palaces such as Knossos on the island of Crete.

The period from 5000 BC to 500 BC produced magnificent buildings, such as the ziggurats of Babylon and the pyramids of Egypt. The stones of Stonehenge and the mysterious heads left by the Olmecs in Central America show that people in Europe and America were also artists and builders.

New technology and ideas

This was an age of crucial new technologies – the wheel, metal tools and weapons were developed at this time. Coins were first used. Writing and mathematics developed. The Babylonians studied the stars. New ideas were developing, and spreading with the help of trade, ready to shape the next stage of human history.

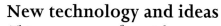

When people settled down to farm
they chose to live near a water supply,
often a river. Between two mighty rivers
– the Tigris and the Euphrates in Mesopotamia – the
world's first great civilization arose 6,000 years ago.

Mesopotamia

Mesopotamia, meaning 'between rivers', lay in the country
we know as modern Iraq. Northern Mesopotamia's weather
was mild, with enough rain for crops to grow in some
areas. In the south lay a flat, swampy plain built up from
mud spread by the river floodwaters. This area was called
Sumer. It had little rain and long, hot summers.

Sumer

People had lived in Sumer since
the 5000s BC. They fished the
rivers, hunted wild pigs and
birds for food, and picked fruit
from date palms. The muddy soil
was rich, but crops died without
rain in the burning summer heat.
So farmers dug canals to channel
river water to their fields of barley,
wheat, dates and vegetables. They
turned over the earth with ploughs
pulled by oxen.

Gods and grain

Farming flourished and by around
3500 BC, new people settled in
Sumer. With their arrival, cities
began to grow. Food was plentiful,
so farming villages grew in number
and size. People lived and worked
together. Their buildings of mud
brick included a house – or temple –
for the local god. Here they offered
gifts in return for the god's care of

The weaving loom is in use by this date. Hot metal working in Near East.	c. 4000 BC
Earliest map on a clay tablet shows River Euphrates.	c. 3800 BC
Towns of Uruk (Eridu) and Ur in Sumer. First use of potter's wheel.	c. 3500 BC
Invention of the wheel in Mesopotamia. Flax grown to make linen.	c. 3500 BC
Cuneiform writing developed in Sumer.	c. 3200 BC
First city states in Mesopotamia and Near East.	c. 3000 BC
Domestication of the horse in central Asia.	c. 2500 BC
Destruction of the city of Ur by the Elamites. The last king of Ur, Ibbi-Sin, is taken captive.	c. 2000 BC

▷ People in
Mesopotamia traded along
the rivers, using small boats.
By 5,000 years ago, people had
invented the wheel, and carts
were pulled by oxen and
donkeys. Sacks of barley were
traded as currency as well as being
used for food.

△ Some of the wedge-shaped ('cuneiform') characters in the Sumerian writing system looked like objects, others were symbols.

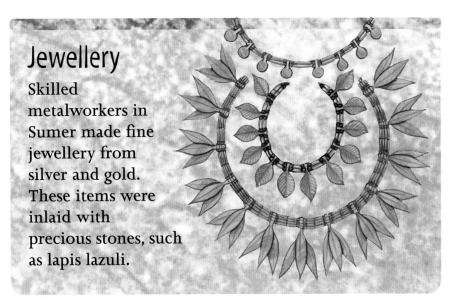

Jewellery

Skilled metalworkers in Sumer made fine jewellery from silver and gold. These items were inlaid with precious stones, such as lapis lazuli.

their families, homes, crops and animals. Gifts of harvest crops led to the temple also being used as a grain store. Even farm animals such as oxen and donkeys were kept there, perhaps to hire out for work in the fields.

Writing and counting

Goods passing in and out of the temple store had to be checked and recorded. A system of numbers and counting was invented – and the world's first writing system. People skilled in writing – the scribes – were highly trained, important people.

The beginning of writing is also the beginning of human history. Sumerians used clay tablets and a sharpened reed to carve wedge-shaped characters into the soft damp surface. The clay was baked hard, so the writing became a permanent record. Sumerian tablets can still be read. The Sumerian system of counting has lasted, too. They used units of 60 when telling the time in seconds, minutes and hours, and when measuring a circle with 360 degrees.

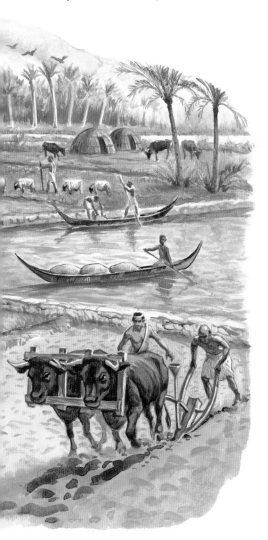

▷ Sumerian women wore long dresses and robes. Rich women liked jewellery, such as bead necklaces, gold earrings and headdresses.

BC

Town life created a society with more rules in which more people did specialized tasks. The world of city-states such as Ur was one run largely by men.

Society and City-states

A man was master of his household, including his wife, children and slaves. Women could, however, own their own property. Boys from wealthier families, such as the sons of court officials, went to school to be taught by scribes. Other children learned to do what their parents did, at home.

Priest power

Priests were important because of the temple trade. They organized everyone who worked in and around the temple, from craftworkers to merchants and scribes. Villagers farmed land for the gods, under the priests' watchful eyes. Farmers paid rent to the temple, and priests also acted as tax collectors. In return, a state allowance of food was distributed to city dwellers.

As villages grew into towns and cities, temple officials played a big part in ruling them. A rich and powerful elite class emerged, living in splendid temple-palaces. Most powerful of all was the king, the gods' representative on earth. He was responsible for law and government, for keeping order and defending civilization against enemies.

City-states and their rulers

Among the earliest cities of southern Mesopotamia were Eridu, Uruk, Nippur and Kish. These were like small states, with their own

First cities of Mesopotamia.	3500 BC
Cities and temples in Sumer built of mud brick.	3000 BC
Rise of city of Ur.	2850 BC
Gilgamesh, legendary ruler.	2750 BC
Rise of the Akkad Empire.	2400 BC
Sargon of Akkad is first great king.	2350 BC
King Ur-Nammu rules Ur.	2112 BC
King Hammurabi rules Babylon.	1750 BC

▷ In Mesopotamia there were hundreds of gods and goddesses, including Nanna the moon god, and Inannna the goddess of love and war.

ENKI

NINHURSAG

NANNA

UTU

INANNA

◁ The royal standard of Ur, a decorated wooden box, dates from about 2500 BC. On its mosaic panels, farmers parade and soldiers march into battle.

△ King Hammurabi of Babylon (ruled c.1792 –1750 BC) is shown before the sun god at the top of this carved stone pillar. The king's laws were carved onto the pillar below.

government and rulers. Around 2700 BC, the title 'lugal', meaning big man, was used for the ruler of Kish. Uruk, which in around 2700 BC was the first city to protect itself with a wall, had a ruler with the title 'En'.

Sargon of Akkad

City-states often fought one another over trade and border disputes. Sumerian soldiers fought mainly on foot, although some rode in chariots drawn by wild asses (onagers). When one city grew powerful enough to rule the others, it created a small kingdom, such as those of Lagash and Ur. Around 2375 BC, Lagash and all the other city-states of Sumer were defeated by Lugalzaggisi, ruler of Umma. Sumer was united under his rule for 25 years. But then from the north came an even mightier conqueror – Sargon of Akkad – the first great king in history.

Sargon created the first empire in Mesopotamia. One of his successors, the fourth king of Akkad, was Naram-Sin (he reigned from 2254 to 2218 BC), whose war triumphs are recorded on a famous sculpture, the Naram-Sin Stele.

Sargon of Akkad

Sargon had been cup-bearer to the king of Kish. Records say that he fought the Sumerian cities, threw down city walls and took 50 of their rulers captive, including the ruler of Uruk. Sargon ruled for a total of 56 years. He made one of his daughters a priestess of the moon god in Ur.

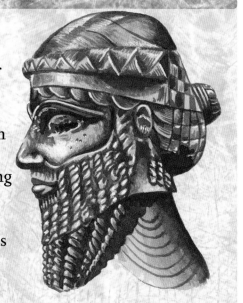

△ In the city-states of Mesopotamia, scribes such as the one shown here carved the local ruler's code of laws onto clay tablets.

In Mesopotamia, as many as 300,000 people lived in a big city. Within the walls, the city was a maze of narrow streets, alleys and marketplaces. Many buildings were made of mud brick, but some houses were built from reeds. They were similar to those still used by people living in southern Iraq.

Homes and Temples

A well-to-do family lived in a two-storey home with no windows. It had a flat roof where the family might sleep, and a central courtyard that was pleasantly cool in the evening. Here, visitors would have their dusty feet washed by a slave. The bedrooms were upstairs; the kitchen, living room and storerooms downstairs. There was little furniture – only chests, stools and tables – and most people slept on mats, although some rich people had beds. Each home had a shrine, set in the wall, and often a small family tomb.

Food and drink

The Sumerians made unleavened bread (bread that does not rise) and ate porridge made from wheat and barley grains. Vegetables, dates, milk, butter and cheese were served at

First cities of Mesopotamia.	3500 BC
Writing in Sumer. First use of bronze.	3200 BC
Cities and temples in Sumer built of mud brick.	3000 BC
Great Pyramid of Giza built in Egypt.	2590 BC

▷ A ziggurat consisted of an enormous platform structure with an earth core, over which unglazed bricks were laid. The building was faced with fire bricks. Ramps and steps led up to the top, where the temple was erected.

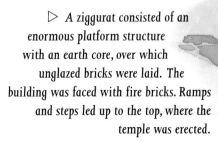

▷ Brick-makers fired bricks in kilns to produce building materials for structures that were intended to last. Kiln-fired bricks could survive the seasonal rains without needing too much repair.

mealtimes too. Cattle and sheep provided meat, and fish was a very popular food. Fish 'take-away' stalls sold ready-cooked fish. The favourite drink was beer. For entertainment, people played board games, listened to stories of legendary heroes or played musical instruments. Water and food were kept in large storage jars. Glass was made, some time before 2000 BC, but for use in jewellery.

Temples to the gods

The Sumerians worshipped many gods and goddesses – gods of the sky, the air, the Sun, the Moon, fertility and wisdom. Each city had its own patron god.

Slaves, taken captive in war, toiled to build Mesopotamia's splendid temples. The White Temple in Uruk, built in the 3000s BC, was made of whitewashed brick, set on top of a pyramid or ziggurat. A ziggurat was an artificial mountain, on which the people thought the local god lived, watching over the citizens he protected. The ziggurat's platform of earth was faced with bricks. Temples were built on top of the platform. The Hanging Gardens of Babylon, one of the Seven Wonders of the Ancient World, were probably built in the same way.

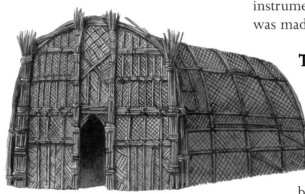

△ Reed houses were built using reeds cut down from the marshes around the Tigris and Euphrates rivers. The Sumerians also made canoes from these reeds.

The wheel

The wheel was first used by the Sumerians in making pottery in about 3500 BC. Around 300 years later this invention was adapted for a startling new use – that of transportation.

△ Mud bricks, dried in the sun, were one of the cheapest building materials. These sun-dried bricks were made stronger with straw, but they were not waterproof.

After the fall of Ur in 2000 BC, many cities of Mesopotamia were ruled by the Amorites, whose two strongholds were Isin and Larsa. In 1763 BC, Larsa fell to a great army led by Hammurabi (1792–1750 BC). The new ruler gave a new name – Babylonia – to the kingdoms of Sumer and Akkad.

Babylonia

Under Hammurabi, all of Mesopotamia came under one rule. The king of Babylonia was also the high priest of the national god. The palace now held power over the temple. Under the king there were three classes of people: aristocrats, commoners and slaves. Trade was no longer controlled by the city, so merchants and traders managed their own businesses.

The laws of Hammurabi

The laws of King Hammurabi applied across his empire. They covered trade, business and prices, family law, criminal law and civil laws. Their main principle was 'the strong shall not injure the weak'. Hammurabi also set up a system of set prices and wages, and gave his people a fair and well-run tax system. In AD 1901 his laws were found written on a stone slab in Susa, Iran – where a victorious king had taken it as war booty.

One of the conflicts between the former

Hittites make iron tools and weapons.	2000 BC
First Babylonian dynasty.	1830 BC
Fall of Larsa. Hammurabi rules Babylon.	1763 BC
Babylon conquers other city-states.	1750 BC
Nebuchadnezzar fights off Assyrian invasion.	1125 BC
Tiglath-pileser I of Assyria conquers Babylon.	1116 BC
Babylon again invaded by Assyrians.	700s BC
Old Babylon falls.	689 BC
Rise of New Babylon.	626 BC

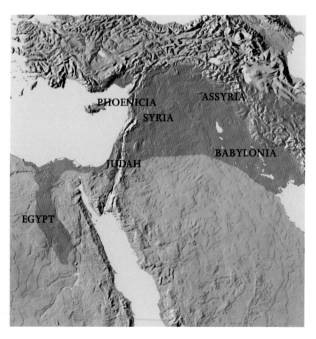

▷ This map shows the extent of the Babylonian Empire under King Nebuchadnezzar II. Under his rule, the Babylonians captured Syria and Palestine.

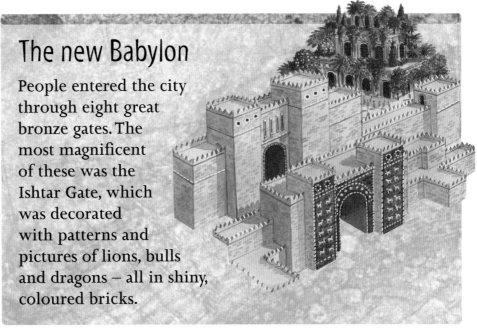

The new Babylon

People entered the city through eight great bronze gates. The most magnificent of these was the Ishtar Gate, which was decorated with patterns and pictures of lions, bulls and dragons – all in shiny, coloured bricks.

△ Marduk was the chief god of Babylonia. Poets praised him as kind and merciful, lord of the heavens and the source of civilization and law. His sacred animals included the dragon.

△ The Babylonians produced written records by carving picture symbols onto clay tablets. The tablets carried information about astronomy and mathematics, as well as records of legal and business matters and religious texts.

states of Babylonia was over the control of river waters. In wartime, rulers dammed rivers to cause flood or drought in the land of their enemies, or a river would be diverted away from the crops of a rival city. Hammurabi now commanded the water power.

Hammurabi's city

The city of Babylon had magnificent temples and palaces. Its winding, narrow streets were lined with private houses. Most had a courtyard with rooms around it. In the city walls were gates, around which traders held markets. Traders and merchants travelled as far afield as Syria, Assyria and the kingdoms of the Persian Gulf.

The fall of Babylon

During the 700s BC Assyrians from the upper Tigris area, north of Babylonia, invaded Babylon. The city was destroyed in 689 BC by the Assyrian king Sennacherib but later rebuilt. A new Babylonian empire began to grow in 626 BC, when the general Nabopolassae defeated the Assyrians. Under this king and his son, Nebuchadnezzar II, the Babylonian Empire controlled most of the Middle East.

▷ The ancient Babylonians were the first to study the stars, some time before 2000 BC. They knew of five planets: Jupiter, Mars, Mercury, Saturn and Venus.

The city-states of Sumer traded across the Arabian Sea with people who lived by another great river – the River Indus which flows through Pakistan. Here one of the world's first great civilizations had begun, like Sumer, with farms, villages and small towns.

The Indus Valley

Farming settlements grow in the Indus Valley.	3000 BC
First cities of the Indus Valley.	2500 BC
Aryans from the north begin to threaten Indus peoples.	2100 BC
Indus Valley civilization starts to decline.	2000 BC
Indus Valley civilization is destroyed.	1500 BC

Around 2500 BC, cities were planned and built. These cities remained unknown until archaeologists began excavating them in the AD 1920s. There were two main cities – Harappa in the north of the Indus Valley and Mohenjo Daro in the south. The people who lived here were farmers, tending fields and watering crops with silt-laden waters washed down when the snows melted in the mountains to the north.

Well-planned cities

Harappa and Mohenjo Daro were carefully planned and laid out on a grid system. They were large cities, over 5 kilometres around their outer boundary. The cities had wide roads and brick houses, most of which

▷ The city of Harappa. Many houses were built on mud-brick platforms to save them from seasonal floods. Most had baths, with water from a public well or a well in the courtyard.

38

Priest kings

Rulers known as priest kings were found in all the great ancient civilizations. This ruler was the link between people and god, on whose will their fate depended. Both Harappa and Mohenjo Daro were probably ruled by a priest king, and by a priestly elite.

△ Archaeologists have found hundreds of artefacts during the excavation of Mohenjo Daro. Many, such as this bronze figurine of a dancing girl, have been well preserved in the sand and mud around the settlement.

△ The farmers of the Indus Valley used wooden carts pulled by a pair of oxen. Deep grooves made by heavily laden carts have been found in the excavated streets of Mohenjo Daro.

had at least two floors. The standards of hygiene and sanitation were high. Many houses had private bathrooms, with pipes leading to main drains under the streets. People also used public wells and baths. Bathing may have been part of certain religious rituals, for which the Great Bath found at Mohenjo Daro probably had a religious function

Traders used a standard system of weights and measures, and each city had a huge granary stocked with grain. Farmers grew wheat, barley, peas, mustard, sesame seeds, dates and cotton. Domesticated animals included dogs, cats, cattle, chickens and possibly pigs, camels, buffalo and elephants. Some of these animals appear on small seals. Over 100 other towns and villages have been found.

Rich from trade

All this suggests a high level of organization. Temples were smaller and less impressive than those of Mesopotamia, but the people of the Indus Valley enjoyed clean and well-run cities. Food was their main export, and trade was carried on by ship with copper producers in the Persian Gulf. Caravans from the north brought silver from Afghanistan and lead from Rajasthan. There was also trade with Sumer, and similarities in art suggest the two cultures copied each other's fashions.

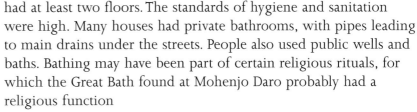

No thing existed, nor did nothing exist:/ there was no air-filled space, no sky beyond./ What held it all? And where? And who secured it?

from THE RIG VEDA, c. 1500 BC

The Rig Veda *is a religious song about the ancient gods of fire, earth, air and water.*

The first great civilization in Europe arose in Greece, around 3000 BC, on the island of Crete in the Mediterranean Sea. It was named 'Minoan' after the legendary King Minos of Crete. In Greek myths, Minos was the son of Europa and Zeus, the king of the gods.

Crete and Mycenae

Earliest settlements on Crete.	*c.* 6000 BC
Stone-built villages on coasts of Crete. Trade with Egypt and Anatolia.	*c.* 3000 BC
Minoan Crete at height of its power. Palace at Knossos.	2000 BC
Start of Mycenean power. Mycenae becomes an important centre.	1900 BC
Mycenae rivals the Minoans of Crete.	1500 BC
Volcanic explosion on island of Thera in *Aegean* Sea.	1470 BC
Myceneans take over Crete. Knossos is destroyed by fire.	1400 BC
Lion gate at Mycenae built.	1300 BC
Collapse of Mycenean civilization.	*c.* 1150 BC

The Cretans were among the first peoples to make bronze tools and weapons. They were farmers and fishing people who lived in small towns or villages protected not by walls or forts but by the sea. These seafarers were the first naval power known in history.

Sailors and traders

The Cretans sailed the Aegean and Mediterranean seas in ships laden with goods produced by the island's farmers and skilled craftworkers – pottery, engraved stone seals, perfumes, metalwork, woollen textiles, olive oil, wine, grain and grapes. Minoan pottery found its way to Egypt, where tomb paintings show Cretans bringing gifts for the pharaoh. They carried tin, gold, pearls and ivory back to Crete. Trade made the Minoans wealthy.

Palace of Knossos

The chief town of Crete was Knossos, where the ruler lived in a luxurious hilltop palace. Courtyards, storehouses and workshops formed part of the palace, which was also the centre of government and an important grain store.

By about 1580 BC, Minoan

▷ The so-called 'mask of *Agamemnon*' was found during the excavation of graves at Mycenae in the late 1800s. Modern historians think the mask belongs to an earlier king.

△ The Minoans favoured goddesses in their worship, including the snake goddess who protected the home. The Cretan civilization left behind a rich legacy of religious belief and tales of heroes and gods.

civilization was spreading to other Aegean islands and to the mainland of Greece. There were palaces in other Minoan towns, such as Mallia and Phaisos. The great palace at Knossos, crushed by an earthquake in 1700 BC, had risen again in even grander form. In about 1450 BC another earthquake hit Crete. After this, the Myceneans – a people from mainland Greece – ruled the island.

Mycenean warriors

The Myceneans were warlike people who lived in Greece, possibly from 1900 BC. By 1600 BC they were trading in the Aegean, and after the fall of Crete they became the major power in the region. They had settlements from Sicily to Syria, and close links with Troy, a city in the rich grain-growing area at the mouth of the Black Sea.

The Mycenean rulers lived in hilltop citadels overlooking cities protected by thick stone walls. The city of Mycenae was at the heart of their civilization. People entered Mycenae through the Lion Gate, a great stone gateway from which a path led straight to the royal palace. Graves of the ruling family, filled with treasure and personal possessions for the afterlife, were found near the gate in AD 1876.

By 1100 BC Mycenean power was over. Raids by pirates cut off Mediterranean trade routes from the Greek mainland. Weakened by interstate warfare, the Mycenean cities were destroyed and lost.

△ Both the Cretans and the Myceneans had forms of writing, which they used in business and government. They wrote on clay tablets and possibly also in ink on papyrus, like the Egyptians. We know of two forms of writing, or scripts, called Linear A and Linear B.

◁ Like other Minoan palaces, the palace at Knossos was designed for elegant living and day-to-day business. Short wooden columns supported the decorated beams of the ceiling.

None of the civilizations in western Europe could rival those of Egypt and the Near East. However, more than 5,000 years ago Europeans were building spectacular stone monuments. Many of these are still standing today, as mysterious relics of a long-gone society.

Megalithic Europe

The huge stones are called megaliths (meaning 'big stones'). Some were set up on their own, others in groups or in circles. Some megaliths marked the burial place of an important ruler, while others seem to have had a religious meaning.

First stone structures in Europe.	4500 BC
Passage graves built at Carnac in France.	4000 BC
Lake villages in central Europe.	3000 BC
Stone temples on the island of Malta.	2800 BC
Beaker Folk begin to settle in Britain.	2500 BC
End of New Stone Age in Britain. First use of bronze.	2000 BC
Earliest work at Stonehenge.	1800 BC
Stonehenge is more or less complete.	1400 BC
Celts begin to settle in Britain.	1000 BC

Europe's population grew as farming developed. People in the north looked southwards towards the Mediterranean for new ideas. Traders from the civilized southern world came as far north as Britain, in search of tin (which was used to make bronze).

Most Europeans lived in small villages, ruled by a chieftain. His power was based on the numbers of weapons, sheep and cattle that he owned. Chieftains controlled trade and the places where people met to do business – river fords, valleys and forest clearings where trails crossed. Travel was difficult because there were no proper roads. Clumsy ox-drawn wagons with iron-rimmed wheels creaked slowly along, carrying heavy goods.

The settlement of Britain

Before 3000 BC, few people lived in the British Isles apart from scattered groups of wandering hunters. Then farmers and herders from

△ Stonehenge was built in stages between 1800 and 1400 BC. During the second stage, blue stones from the Preseli Mountains in Wales were hauled onto the site in an astonishing feat of organization and transport. Local stones added in the third stage were up to 10 metres long and weighed 50 tonnes.

Stone relics

Rock tombs, slab tombs such as this dolmen (right) and stone circles and temples lie scattered across Europe, even on the island of Malta. The work of trimming and raising the stones was highly skilled.

mainland Europe arrived. They brought cattle, sheep and pigs, and began to clear the forests to grow crops.

From about 2500 BC new migrants arrived, bringing with them bronze tools and a distinctive pottery. Historians call them the 'Beaker Folk'. They mined copper and tin, made gold jewellery and wove wool and linen for clothing.

Mound diggers and stone movers

People had no machines, and yet they tackled huge digging works. They buried their chieftains, with treasures and food for the next world, beneath mounds of earth called barrows. Many of these barrows can still be seen.

Tall single stones (menhirs), stone slab-tombs (dolmens) and the remains of large circles of stones and wooden posts (henges) are also still standing. In Britain, the most impressive stone circles are at Avebury and Stonehenge in Wiltshire. At Carnac, in northern France, there are avenues of standing stones.

Iron Age Europe

The Stonehenge builders had only stone or bronze tools. The Iron Age began in central Europe about 1000 BC. Early iron-using people mined salt as well as iron ore. About 1000 BC, new settlers called Celts came to Britain from mainland Europe. These newcomers were iron-makers and fort-builders.

△ Many people in Britain and Europe lived in village communities. A typical village dwelling consisted of a round wooden framework, filled in with twigs, turf and mud, with a thatched roof.

▷ The Celts were skilled craftworkers, making highly decorated ornaments out of bronze and iron. Their work featured elaborate and distinctive patterns of interwoven curves and spirals.

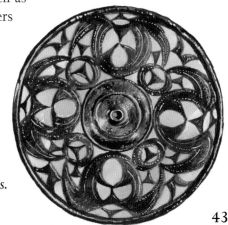

BC

2,000 BC · 400,000 BC · 100,000 BC · 20,000 BC · 10,000 BC · 4,000 BC

For most of a period lasting 3,000 years Egypt was the strongest power in the world. It ruled an empire which at its peak in about 1500 BC included Palestine and Syria. Egyptians kings, or pharaohs, built the greatest monuments of the ancient world – the Pyramids.

Egypt

Egyptian armies fought off invaders and conquered new lands, while traders journeyed across the Mediterranean Sea and southwards into Africa to bring back treasures to add to Egypt's wealth. This wealth was based on a river – the mighty Nile. The Egyptians called their land Kemet ('black land'). Each year, the Nile flooded and its waters spilled over the banks to spread a layer of black, fertile mud on the fields where the farmers grew their crops. This yearly gift of the Nile allowed people to enjoy civilization and plenty.

Egypt united

The earliest peoples of Egypt were desert nomads. As they settled to become farmers, they built villages and towns. By 3100 BC, Egypt had become one country. The southern kingdom of Upper Egypt conquered the northern kingdom of Lower Egypt, and King Menes made Memphis his capital.

The Egyptians regarded their king as a god. Thirty dynasties (ruling families) of these god-kings ruled from the time of King Menes in 3100 BC until 332 BC when Alexander the Great conquered Egypt. From about 1554 BC the Egyptian kings were given the title pharaoh.

First dynastic period. Egypt is united under one king.	3100 BC
Old Kingdom. The Pyramids are built at Giza.	2686–2160 BC
A period of unrest and famine. Pyramids are robbed.	2160–2040 BC
Middle Kingdom. Capital of Egypt moves to Thebes. Strong pharaohs rule.	2040–1786 BC
Hyksos people from the north invade.	1786 BC
New Kingdom. Amenhotep IV becomes king (1367).	1567–1085 BC
Rameses III fights off invasions by Sea Peoples.	1179 BC
The Late Dynastic Period. Libyan and Nubian pharaohs rule.	1085–332 BC
Egypt becomes part of the Roman Empire.	30 BC

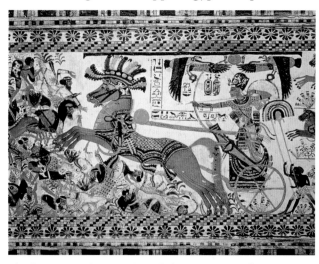

△ This picture shows a pharaoh firing an arrow from his battle chariot. It is part of a decorative scene on the side of a chest found in the tomb of the boy-king Tutankhamun.

▷ The Nile not only provided Egypt's people with rich, fertile soil and plentiful water, but it was also a source of food. Egyptians caught river fish to add to their basic diet. They used spears to hunt ducks on the river too.

△ The shaduf was a bucket swung from the end of a counterweighted pole. It was used to lift water from irrigation ditches, and is still used in Egypt today.

Government and daily life

Egypt was governed by officials and tax collectors, who measured the Nile's waters to predict how high it would flood each year, and so how big a harvest was to be expected. Taxes were set accordingly.

Most Egyptians were farmers. They grew crops of barley, wheat, fruit and vegetables. Their diet consisted of daily meals of bread and beer, often supplemented with fish. Meat from cattle, sheep and goats was a luxury.

Children began work at the age of five. Boys went to school if their parents could afford to spare them from work, and some girls did too. There were many slaves, but even freemen might be press-ganged to dig irrigation canals, or haul stones to building sites. Skilled workers, such as scribes (writers), stone-cutters, carpenters, metalworkers, painters, potters, bakers and brewers, were kept busy in the towns.

The Egyptians were good at maths, particularly at geometry, which they used in architecture and surveying. They drew up an accurate 12-month calendar of 365 days, and used water clocks to measure time.

Picture-writing

Egyptian picture-writing is known as hieroglyphics. It was made up of about 750 signs, with pictures of people, animals and objects. Scribes used a quick form of writing called hieratic.

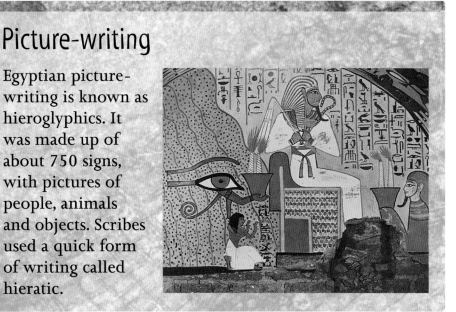

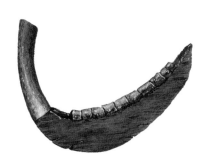

△ Egyptian farmers used sickles to harvest their crops. The harvest period traditionally lasted from March to July. Other farm equipment included ox-drawn wooden ploughs which were used to prepare the soil before planting time.

Religion played an important part in Egyptian life. The Egyptians believed in many gods and goddesses. Their chief deities were Ra the sun god, Horus the sky god, Osiris the god of the underworld, and Isis, wife of Osiris, who represented the ideal woman.

Pyramids and Gods

This large group of gods was challenged on only one occasion, when the pharaoh Amenhotep tried to introduce worship of one supreme being, the sun god Aton.

Town gods and temples

Gods looked after every aspect of life. Every town and city had its own god, too. Temples were dedicated to a particular god or a dead pharaoh. The biggest of all these temples was the temple of Amun (a sun god who came to be linked with Ra) at Karnak. The pharaoh was the chief priest as well as a god himself. Priests in each temple cared for the statue of the god that was kept there, washing it and offering it gifts of food. Priests also prayed to the gods. Ordinary people said their prayers in the home.

The next world and mummies

The Egyptians believed in an afterlife, to which human souls journeyed after death. They thought it important that the bodies of the dead should be preserved for life in the next world, and so they developed techniques for making 'mummies'.

The dead person's organs were removed and the body was embalmed and dried,

First 'step' pyramid at Saqqara, built by Imhotep for the pharaoh Zoser.	2780 BC
Great Pyramid at Giza built for the pharaoh Cheops (Khufu).	2700 BC
The pharaohs stop building pyramids. Later kings are buried in rock tombs.	1700 BC
Start of reign of pharaoh Amenhotep III – a great age for Egypt.	1420 BC
Temples at Luxor built.	1400 BC
Reign of Amenhotep IV who tries to introduce the worship of one sun god.	1367 BC
Tutankhamun rules. Egypt returns to the old gods.	1347 BC
Temples at Abu Simbel are built during the reign of Rameses II.	1280 BC

▷ The Great Sphinx is a mysterious rock sculpture, with a human head on the body of a lion. Some historians believe it is older than the Pyramids.

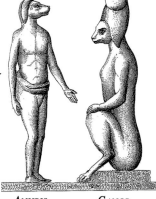

▷ Many Egyptian gods were pictured with animal heads. Horus, son of Isis and Osiris, was shown with a falcon's head. Anubis, god of death, had the head of a jackal.

ISIS   AMUN   OSIRIS   SERVANT   ANUBIS   CANOP

△ The sun god Ra was often portrayed simply as a sun disk. He appeared in other forms too, including a cat, a bird and a lion.

using salts and chemicals, and wrapped in linen bandages. It was then placed in a coffin. Even animals such as cats and monkeys were sometimes mummified. Many thousands of mummies must have been made, but only about 1,000 survive today.

Pyramids and rock tombs

Pyramids are the oldest stone structures in the world. There are more than 30, but the most famous are the three Great Pyramids at Giza. The biggest, which was built for the pharaoh Cheops, contains about two million blocks of limestone and is 140 metres high.

The pyramids were built as tombs, to keep the body of the dead king safe for eternity and perhaps (through their sky-pointing shape) to ease his passage to the heavens. The work of building such enormous monuments must have taken years, even with as many as 100,000 workers toiling to move the huge stone blocks up sloping ramps of sand.

Mighty as they were, the pyramids were not able to keep out human robbers. The treasures left inside each burial chamber with the king were invariably stolen.

Tutankhamun

Tutankhamun became king of Egypt at the age of 9 and died when he was about 18. His tomb is one of more than 60 royal tombs around the Valley of the Kings. Its four rooms contained more than 5,000 objects – from ostrich feathers and model ships to a throne and a gold death mask.

△ Osiris, god of the dead, was often shown as a mummy on a throne, wearing the crown of Upper Egypt.

47

BC/AD

Abraham was the founder of the Hebrew people, according to the Bible. In about 1850 BC he lived in the Sumerian city of Ur. Forced to leave his homeland because of unrest and war, he led his family northeast along the course of the Euphrates, and then west to settle in the land of Canaan.

The Jews

Abraham journeys to Canaan.	*c.*1850 BC
Probable date of Exodus from Egypt.	1250 BC
Philistines conquer Israel.	1050 BC
Saul chosen as king.	1020 BC
King David unites the people. His son Solomon builds the Temple in Jerusalem.	1010 BC
After the death of Solomon ten northern tribes break away.	938 BC
Babylonians conquer Judah.	604 BC
Romans conquer Judah.	63 BC
Temple in Jerusalem is destroyed.	AD 66

The Bible records that Abraham had two sons, Ishmael (the ancestor of the Arabs) and Isaac. Isaac had two sons, Esau and Jacob, and Jacob (also called Israel) had 12 sons. These sons became the heads of the Twelve Tribes, the Israelites of the Bible.

Exile in Egypt and Moses

One of Jacob's sons, Joseph, led the Israelites into Egypt after famine struck the land of Canaan. The Israelites became wealthy and influential, but under the rule of successive Egyptian pharaohs the Israelites were forced into slavery. This slavery lasted until about 1250 BC, when Moses was commanded by God to lead the Israelites out of Egypt in what became known as the Exodus.

Moses was the great law-giver of Jewish history and religion. Jews believe that he received the Ten Commandments from God, and taught his people to believe in one God. This belief in one God became the central pillar of the Jewish faith (and later of Christianity and Islam). Moses led the Israelites through the desert to Canaan, where they settled with the local Canaanites and Philistines. For a time,

▷ In this dramatic picture, the Israelites are conquering the city of Jericho; at God's command the walls tumble down at the sound of the Israelite army shouting and banging drums.

▷ Moses, the leader of the Hebrew people, receives the two tablets from God. The stone tablets bear the Ten Commandments, as described in the Old Testament. They became the basis for Jewish law.

△ Jews believe that the Dome of the Rock, in Jerusalem, is built over the rock on which Abraham, on God's orders, prepared to sacrifice his son Isaac. Muslims believe that Muhammad rose to heaven from the same rock.

chosen men and women called judges led the tribes, but in about 1020 BC the judge Samuel chose Saul to be the first king of Israel.

Israel and Judah

The Israelites settled in the hills of Canaan. The towns were held by their enemies, the Canaanites and Philistines. The Israelites, under King David, defeated the Philistines. After the death of Solomon, David's son, the kingdom split. Two southern tribes formed their own kingdom, Judah. The northern kingdom of Israel was more powerful, but was weakened by royal squabbles and fierce religious disputes. The Assyrians overran Israel in 721 BC. It was crushed by Babylon in 604 BC, and most of the people were taken as slaves.

Exile and conquest

During this exile in Babylon much of the Bible (Old Testament) took on the form it takes today. In 538 BC the Persian king Cyrus, conqueror of Babylon, allowed the exiles to leave. Later, Judah became part of the Greek Empire. In 63 BC the Romans conquered Judah, calling it Judea. In AD 66 the Jews rose in revolt, and the Romans retaliated by destroying the Temple.

King Solomon

Solomon was the son of David, the greatest Israelite king who ruled from 1010 to 970 BC. David defeated the Philistines and enlarged the kingdom, making Jerusalem his capital city. Solomon saw to the building of the Temple in Jerusalem, the most sacred centre of the Jewish religion. After Solomon's death Israel split into two separate kingdoms.

△ The Dead Sea scrolls are ancient documents written on leather and copper. They contain the oldest known handwritten texts of books of the Bible.

BC

The Phoenicians lived along the shores of the eastern Mediterranean (roughly where Lebanon is today). They were the most famous seamen of the ancient world. From the 1200s BC, Phoenicians made trade voyages across the Mediterranean and set up colonies as far away as Morocco and Spain.

Phoenicia and Assyria

The Phoenicians built strong, single-masted ships, with a large sail, and oars for use in windless conditions or river estuaries. When in unfamiliar territory, the Phoenicians would anchor offshore, land and set out their goods in 'silent trade' with local people.

Assyria independent under King Shamshi-Adad.	1810 BC
Assyrian power great, then declines.	1230s BC
Rise of Phoenicians. Tyre is an important city.	1200 BC
First Phoenician colony in North Africa, at Utica.	1140 BC
Assyrian power recovers. They conquer Babylon.	1116 BC
Rise of Carthage.	750 BC
Assyrians attack Babylon.	729 BC
Sargon II starts to build palace at Khorsabad.	721 BC
End of Assyrian Empire.	612 BC
Nineveh destroyed by Medes, Babylonians and Scythians.	609 BC

Their voyages took them beyond the Mediterranean, into the Atlantic Ocean. As explorers and traders, they helped to spread geographical and scientific knowlege. Their fleet was a powerful war weapon, and Phoenician ships were hired by the Persians to attack Greece.

Phoenician colonies

The most famous Phoenician colony was Carthage, in North Africa. Founded some time before 750 BC, Carthage was one of the great cities of the ancient world, with a harbour big enough for hundreds of ships. Its downfall came after a series of wars against the Greeks, and final defeat by the Romans in the Punic Wars (264–146 BC).

▷ A Phoenician trading ship at a Mediterranean port. On the quayside, a scribe records the shipment as jars of oil, dye and textiles are unloaded. In the background is a war galley with oars and a ram for attacking enemy ships.

Ashurbanipal

From 668 to 627 BC, Assyria was ruled by a king called Ashurbanipal. He was the last great Assyrian ruler. Ashurbanipal made the city of Nineveh his capital. Here, he oversaw the building of a magnificent palace and library and ornate gardens.

△ The Phoenicians were famous for the red-purple colour of their textiles. They used a dye extracted from molluscs. The name 'Phoenician' comes from a Greek word meaning red-purple.

The Assyrians

The Assyrians lived in the northern part of Mesopotamia (what is now northern Iraq). Their homeland was around the upper Tigris River. They were farmers who dug irrigation ditches to water their crops, the most important of which was barley. Numbers of people roamed the land more or less as bandits, and many more fought as soldiers. The Assyrians were feared throughout the Middle East as conquerors.

The rise of the Assyrians began in the 1800s BC. They expanded their trade networks as far as the Mediterranean, but were checked by the strength of the Babylonian king Hammurabi. By about the 800s BC, they had a formidable army of cavalry, infantry and archers. The Assyrians were expert at capturing towns, using wooden siege towers from which to scale or batter down the walls. They earned a reputation for extreme cruelty, slaughtering captives and looting from the peoples they defeated.

The Assyrian chief god was Assur, and the king was Assur's representative on Earth. The king was in charge of the army and the government, and he also controlled the temples and their priests. The Assyrians built on an impressive scale, constructing magnificent temples and palaces in cities such as Assur and Nineveh. Their greatest building was probably the citadel of King Sargon II, in Khorsabad, built in the late 700s BC.

◁ Assyrian artists made wall relief sculptures showing winged spirits, hunting scenes, lions and bulls. For sport, the Assyrian king and his nobles would kill captive lions released into special enclosures.

BC

4,000 BC
2,000 BC
400,000 BC
100,000 BC
20,000 BC
10,000 BC

People had already lived in China for at least 500,000 years when farming began in the valleys of the Huang He (Yellow) and other rivers, more than 5,000 years ago.

China's Early Rulers

From a hazy mixture of history and legend, we learn that China's first ruling family was the Hsia. The legendary first emperors are said to have tamed the rivers, so that farmers could grow millet and wheat.

The first rulers known from archaeological evidence were the Shang. From about 1500 BC, they controlled the best farmland – around the Huang He valley – and from here their power spread.

Shang splendour

The Shang kings were cruel, ruling in barbaric splendour. They built China's first cities. Shang bronzesmiths were expert at making cooking pots, tools and weapons. Slave workers sweated to dig enormous pit tombs for dead kings, who were buried with treasures, chariots and horses, and dozens of slain servants and soldiers to accompany their master into the next world. Farmers supplied food to the local nobleman, in return for protection.

The Zhou invaders

Shang rule lasted until 1122 BC. By then, according to Chinese histories, the rulers had become tyrants. The Zhou from the west invaded and overthrew the last

First farming villages in river valleys.	c. 3000 BC
Traditional date for the discovery of silk by the wife of a Chinese emperor.	2690 BC
Legendary dynasty of Hsia.	2200 BC
China's first kings, the Shang. Use of bronze tools.	1500 BC
The city of Anyang becomes the capital of China.	1500 BC
Zhou dynasty.	1122 BC
Period of unrest and civil wars.	770 BC
First emperor, Shih Huang-di of the Qin.	221 BC
Work starts on Great Wall to keep out the Hsiung-nu (Huns).	214 BC

▷ Ordinary people lived in villages, growing cereals and raising chickens, pigs, sheep and cattle. They used oxen and water buffalo to pull ploughs, and dug ditches to water their fields.

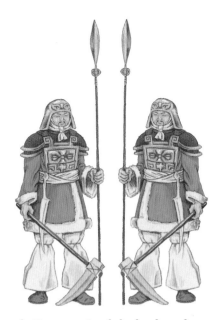

Chinese writing

An example of Chinese writing on silk. The Chinese wrote in picture signs, and made up about 50,000 characters. The first important work of Chinese literature – a collection of poems – dates from before 1000 BC.

△ Fierce warriors helped to keep the Shang rulers, China's first dynasty, in power for more than 400 years.

△ This food vessel, from the time of the Shang dynasty, is decorated with intricate animal motifs. It is in the form of a tiger protecting the body of a man.

Shang king. The new kings were backed by powerful nobles. Nobles built forts and walled towns to defend their lands against one another. They also fought off fierce nomads who swept down from the northern steppes on sturdy horses.

Warring states

No Zhou ruler was strong enough to control all China. For 500 years small warring states fought for power. Yet still China prospered. Farmers grew more food and metalworkers mastered the new skills of making iron tools. Potters, jewellers, tailors and chariot-makers were kept busy. Scholars attended the nobles' courts, seeking work as government officials. Trade grew and people began to use money.

The first emperor

The Qin ruler Shih Huang-di fought his way to power as first emperor of all China in 221 BC. He crushed the power of the nobles, handing over the government to hired officials (who did what he told them). He ordered everyone to speak the same language, and to use the same weights and measures. Thousands of people were forced into work-gangs to build new roads and canals, and the emperor also built the Great Wall, which linked up older walls to create the biggest frontier defence on the Earth.

◁ The Shang kings were superstitious. They consulted 'oracle bones' before making any important decision. A soothsayer would read the signs in animal bones cracked by heat, and advise the king accordingly.

War has been a part of life for as long as humans have existed. Prehistoric people fought for territory and food, using rocks and sticks as weapons. Later, they used stone-tipped spears and bows and arrows.

War and Weapons

The discovery of bronze in about 3500 BC brought the first revolution in weaponry. Bronze swords and spear points were sharper than stone and bone weapons. Iron was even stronger still. Peoples of the Near East, such as the Hittites, were the first to master iron-making.

Armies and armour

Each of the ancient Near East superpowers rounded up civilians to serve in armies for the conquest of other countries, and for defence against enemies. To protect themselves, soldiers began wearing armour on their bodies. By the time of the Trojan War, about 1200 BC, armour was made from metal plates fastened with leather thongs. Soldiers

A sculpture shows an Egyptian king pictured defeating an enemy.	3100 BC
Sumerians make bronze war axes and spear points.	2500 BC
Body armour used by Egyptians and Mesopotamians.	2000 BC
Chariots in use in Egypt and Near East. Sickle-shaped swords of bronze.	1500 BC
First iron swords. End of Trojan War.	1200 BC
Assyrian armies include infantry, cavalry and chariots.	800 BC
Chainmail made from iron links replaces bronze armour.	500 BC
Sparta has the first full-time army in the Greek world.	400s BC

▷Assyrian troops used wheeled siege towers with iron-tipped rams to batter down the walls of enemy towns.

△ Egyptian soldiers fought with spears, axes, clubs, javelins (throwing spears) swords and bows and arrows. Trumpeters blew signal calls to direct the troops.

△ Axe heads were made from bronze (shown here) and iron. A popular weapon, particularly among Chinese troops, was a halberd, a long spear with an axelike head.

Hittite charioteers

The Hittites, a fierce people from Anatolia (modern Turkey), were the first to use chariots in war. Hittite archers fired their arrows from these chariots, giving them a great advantage over the enemy.

wore metal helmets to protect the head, and carried shields (usually round or rectangular). Some warriors scorned armour – the Greeks and Celts sometimes fought practically naked.

The first organized armies

Kings had small bodyguards of trained soldiers, including chariot-drivers, but they still relied on untrained peasants as foot soldiers. The Assyrians organized the first 'professional' army, and were greatly feared because of its ferocity. An Assyrian army included cavalry (soldiers on horses) and infantry (soldiers on foot).

Assyrian soldiers wore chainmail armour, and fought with iron swords and spears. Archers rode into battle on chariots, then sheltered behind basketwork shields to fire and reload. Slingers hurled stones, often farther than a javelin.

Infantry and cavalry

In China, soldiers traditionally fought on foot, and in huge armies (as many as 100,000 men). Facing marauders on horseback, the Chinese had to become horse-soldiers too. The Chinese composite bow of wood and bone had a longer range than a simple bow. Chinese archers also used crossbows.

There was the clash of shields, of spears and the fury of men cased in bronze... then there were mingled the groaning and the crowing of men killed and killing.

from THE ILIAD, HOMER (8TH CENTURY BC)

Nothing is known about Homer for certain. Tradition states he lived near Greece and wrote two great poems about the Trojan wars: The Iliad *and* The Odyssey.

Other civilizations of Africa were developing to the south of Egypt. These peoples traded with the land of the pharaohs, and with each other along the rivers and across the mighty Sahara Desert.

African Civilizations

Before 6000 BC, the Sahara had a wetter climate than now. The herders and hunters who lived among its lakes left rock paintings showing a Saharan grassland and wildlife very different from the desert of today. About 3500 BC, the Sahara began to dry up, but people still followed old trade routes across the spreading desert.

Rivers and lakes in Sahara start to dry up as climate changes.	3500 BC
Origins of Kush.	2000 BC
Sahara is a desert. Egyptians invade Kush.	1500 BC
Iron-working in northern Africa.	1000 BC
Traditional date for founding of Carthage.	814 BC
Kush throws off Egyptian rule. Kushites conquer Egypt.	750 BC
Nok culture in West Africa. Iron-working spreads into east Africa.	500 BC
Kushite city of Meroe at its finest.	300 BC

A network of trade routes linked the peoples of West Africa with others in the Nile Valley and in North Africa. In Africa, the Stone Age and Iron Age overlapped. Herders became ironsmiths, moving with their herds and tools and spreading the use of iron across Africa.

Kingdom of Kush

The kingdom of Kush was in Nubia (modern Sudan). It lay in the shadow of Egypt and was at first ruled by Egyptians. Its chief cities were Napata on the River Nile, and later Meroe, a city which grew in importance because iron was mined close by. Meroe was impressive, with stone and brick palaces, baths and the temple of the Kush lion-god Apedemeck. Kushite kings were buried in pyramid-shaped tombs beside the Nile.

△ Many of the African kingdoms and peoples traded with the Egyptians to the north. Egyptian traders wanted copper, ivory and ebony, animal skins, cattle – and slaves. They paid for these goods with gold, barley, wheat and papyrus.

△ *A section of a wall painting from a tomb of ancient Egypt. It shows a group of Nubians offering various gifts to the Egyptian pharaoh.*

Carthage

The city-state of Carthage had two large harbours, crammed with naval and trading vessels. It was overlooked by the Byrsa, a huge walled fortress on the hill above.

The Nok people

South and west of the great desert, trade caravans carrying salt and slaves across the Sahara gathered at small towns. The market towns grew into cities and some, such as Djenne in Mali, still thrive.

The Niger River valley was the home of the Nok people. Their society developed from about 500 BC Most people were farmers, but others were merchants, ironsmiths and craftworkers. Each town had its own king. He ruled over a community of large family groups, in which three or four generations lived together. Temples honoured ancestors and heroes. Nok artists made elegant clay heads and figures of people.

The city-state of Carthage

Before the rise of Rome, the city-state of Carthage, in what is now Tunisia, ruled the Mediterranean. Traditionally founded in 814 BC by Phoenicians from Tyre, Carthage grew rich on trade.

The Carthaginians were daring seamen, sailing their oared ships across the Mediterranean and into the Atlantic. An explorer named Hanno is said to have sailed as far south as the Guinea coast of West Africa. Carthage remained rich and powerful for 600 years, until it challenged Rome in three costly wars – and lost.

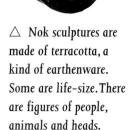

△ *Nok sculptures are made of terracotta, a kind of earthenware. Some are life-size. There are figures of people, animals and heads.*

Carthage had wealth and power; and it had skill and ferocity in war. Juno is said to have loved Carthage best of all cities in the world.

THE AENEID, VIRGIL (70-19 BC)

Virgil's Aeneid *tells the story of Aeneas, who visited Carthage before he founded the city of Rome.*

The first Americans, having crossed from Asia, lived as wandering hunters or settled along the coasts in fishing communities. Groups of people carried on southwards, through the forests and prairies, across the jungles and mountains of Panama, and into the grasslands, rainforests and mountains of South America.

The Americas

Many of these first Americans continued to live as hunter-gatherers. Some became farmers, and settled in villages which grew into towns. Two groups developed America's earliest civilizations – in Mesoamerica (Mexico and Central America) and in Peru on the west coast of South America.

The Olmecs of Mesoamerica

The Olmecs flourished between about 1200 and 400 BC. They made pottery, and cleared the jungle to grow crops. They travelled along rivers on rafts and canoes and settled near rivers. These villages grew to become the first towns in Mexico and Central America. The Olmecs believed in nature gods of the forest and of fertility, and in their towns they built earth mounds with straw and mud temples on top to worship these gods.

Farmers grew corn, chillies, beans and squash. People also collected shellfish and hunted forest animals with spears and nets. Olmec society was ruled by a small group of priest-nobles, who carried out temple ceremonies, owned the best farmland, and controlled trade in valuable raw materials, such as jade.

Stone Age hunters move into the Andes Mountains.	8000 BC
People in Peru grow beans, corn and other crops.	7000 BC
Cotton weaving begins in Peru.	2500 BC
First Mayan languages – in Mexico.	2500 BC
Religious centres, with stone temples, built in Peru.	2000 BC
First use of iron in South America.	c. 1500 BC
Growth of settlements in Olmec region.	1200–900 BC
Rise of Chavin civilization.	1000 BC
Gold-working is widespread in South America.	800 BC

▷ The Olmec people constructed large stepped pyramids from earth. They held religious ceremonies and worshipped their gods in temples built on top of these pyramids.

▷ In modern Peru, craftworkers carry on the traditions of their Chavin ancestors, producing colourful handwoven textiles. Designs such as these have been produced in Peru for around 3,000 years.

△ The mysterious stone head sculptures made by the Olmecs may have been totems, to protect the people against enemies or natural disaster. Using stone chisels and hammers, the Olmec people worked on their sculptures in teams.

Stone heads and sacrifices

The most remarkable Olmec remains are huge stone heads, some two metres high, and other carvings of human figures with flattened features. They may represent human sacrifices. Prisoners taken in war, or contestants in a ritual ball game, may have been killed as sacrifices to the Olmec jaguar-god. Carvings show priests wearing jaguar masks. Some symbols cut into stones may be numbers, suggesting the Olmecs perhaps had a calendar.

Civilizations of Peru

In South America, people living in the Andes foothills had become farmers by about 1000 BC. They built the first towns in South America. One of the earliest civilizations of the Andes was Chavin de Huantar in Peru.

Like the Olmecs, the Chavins were ruled by priests, who later became nobles serving a king. They set up rows of stone pillars that look like ceremonial routes. They also carved stone heads and sculptures of jaguars, snakes and condors. The Chavins used wool from alpacas and vicunas to weave textiles. Although they had only stone tools, they made beautiful gold, silver and copper jewellery.

Chavin farmers

The Chavin people grew corn, potatoes and peppers. They cut terraces into hillsides and became expert at irrigation (channelling water) to cultivate the dry land and mountain slopes. Families kept llamas, guinea pigs and dogs for meat.

△ An Olmec figurine carved from jade. Skilled craftworkers made carvings and sculptures from stone, clay and jade.

By about 1000 BC, the civilizations of North Africa and the Near East had begun to exchange ideas. These civilizations were linked by trading routes. New ideas travelled between civilizations as groups of peoples moved around the world, for trade and also for conquest.

Empires East and West

People moved overland with their animal herds or set sail in ships to settle in new lands. In Egypt, China, India and Mesopotamia civilization had introduced new ways of life. These involved farming, living in towns, trade, organized religion and government by kings. The people who shared these common experiences were more likely to adapt to life under a common ruler, and this encouraged the growth of new empires.

Building empires

These empires brought together different peoples who spoke different languages and sometimes lived far apart. Strong rulers, backed by powerful armies, struggled to win empires and then hold them together. Sometimes the unifying force in building an empire was the will of a dynamic ruler, such

as Alexander the Great. At other times it was the power of armies, religious zeal or the attraction of a way of life that offered greater peace and prosperity for all.

America, Australasia and Africa south of the Sahara were still untouched by the civilizations of Europe and Asia. However, as contacts between the empires of the East and the West grew, the chain of civilization added new links. By about AD 100, when the Roman Empire was at its height, civilization in one form or another existed from western Europe across to China in the East.

Cultural areas

The empires of Greece, Asoka's India, Han China and Rome created 'cultural areas' that were larger than any in earlier history. Inside these empires ideas, knowledge, religious beliefs and culture could spread and take root. Their effect on the history of the world has been to leave behind a cultural legacy that is still very much part of our lives today.

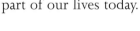

BC

Persia grew from the rubble of the defeated Assyrian Empire. In 612 BC Nineveh, the Assyrian capital, fell. This left Babylon and Media to wrestle over the remains of the empire.

The Persian Empire

In 550 BC the Persian king Cyrus defeated the Medes and made himself ruler of a new empire. It was known as the Achaemenid Empire, after an ancestor of Cyrus who was named Achaemenes.

The Persians

The Persians were Iranians, whose ancestors had ridden on horses from the plains of central Asia. Many Persians lived as nomads, but their rulers built mighty cities with stone palaces. The greatest Persian city was Persepolis, built to the orders of the king, Darius I, in about 518 BC. A Persian man could have several wives, but the king could marry only women selected from six noble families.

The god of light

The Persians believed in sun and sky gods, and gods of nature. They built no temples, but worshipped on the tops of mountains. The chief

Medes set up a kingdom in what is now Iran.	700 BC
Cyrus the Great rebels against the Medes. Achaemenid Empire founded.	550 BC
Cyrus conquers Lydia.	545 BC
Cambyses, son of Cyrus, defeats the Egyptian king Psamtik III.	525 BC
Darius I becomes ruler of Persia.	522 BC
Battle of Marathon halts Persian invasion of Greece.	490 BC
Battles of Thermopylae and Salamis. Greeks defeat Xerxes, son of Darius I.	480 BC
Alexander the Great conquers Persia.	331 BC

△ The ruins of Persepolis, the capital of the Persian Empire, lie near the modern city of Shiraz, in southwest Iran. Part of the ruined palace of Darius I is still standing.

△ Ten thousand soldiers called the Immortals formed the core of the Persian army. Each spearman or archer was instantly replaced if killed or sick.

Mithra

Although Ahura Mazda was the chief god of Persia, many people also worshipped Mithra, seen here killing a bull as a sacrifice to renew life. Later, Mithraism was popular among the Romans.

△ Darius I ruled Persia from 521 to 486 BC. He encouraged trade through the use of coins and new canals.

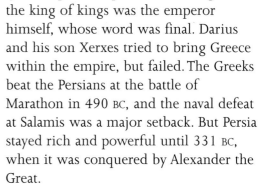

god of Persia was Ahura Mazda, a winged god of light. Many people followed the teachings of the prophet Zarathustra (Zoroaster), who lived between 1400 and 1000 BC. He taught that life was a struggle between good (light) and evil (darkness).

War and empire

The Persians were good fighters, with cavalry and iron weapons, and their military energy proved too strong for their neighbours. The great soldier Cyrus conquered Lydia and the Greek colonies in Asia Minor, and won control of Babylon, too. When he died, his son Cambyses conquered Egypt. Civil war broke out after Cambyses' death, but order was restored by Darius, a relative of Cambyses.

The wars with Greece

Darius was an able administrator. He organized the empire into provinces, each governed by a satrap. A satrap was like a king, but the king of kings was the emperor himself, whose word was final. Darius and his son Xerxes tried to bring Greece within the empire, but failed. The Greeks beat the Persians at the battle of Marathon in 490 BC, and the naval defeat at Salamis was a major setback. But Persia stayed rich and powerful until 331 BC, when it was conquered by Alexander the Great.

◁ The Persian Empire stretched from North Africa as far as the Caucasus Mountains in the north, and the borders of India in the east.

Ancient Greece, practically cut off by sea from Asia Minor (Turkey), had escaped conquest by the warlike empires of the Near East. In this land of mountains and plains, small city-states grew up independent and proud.

The Rise of Greece

Farmland was so scarce that many Greeks left home and wandered in search of new lands. They built fine oared ships, and Greek colonists and traders could be found from one end of the Mediterranean Sea to the other.

Greek cities

Living in their small cities, the Greeks developed a remarkable system of government. Each city was enclosed by a wall for protection. Inside the city was a fort, called an *acropolis*, on a hill or mountain top. An open space, the *agora*, was used as a market and meeting place, where the men of the city met to agree how they should be governed.

Athens and Sparta

The two states of Athens and Sparta became rivals. Athens was rich and cultured. Its citizens included astronomers, mathematicians, thinkers, writers and artists. This was a society with slaves, but its finest rulers, such as Pericles (from about 495 to 429 BC) had vision, and its government was the first real democracy – although only men could take part.

Mycenean culture draws to a close in Greece.	1200 BC
First recorded Olympic Games.	776 BC
Nobles overthrow kings in city-states.	750 BC
Greeks found colonies around the Mediterranean Sea.	500s BC
Athens becomes a democracy, with a council of 500 men to govern it.	508 BC
Greeks defeat Persian invasions.	490–479 BC
Start of Athens' Golden Age under Pericles.	477 BC
War between Sparta and Athens, won by Sparta.	431–404 BC

▷ In 480 BC the Greek fleet defeated the Persians at the battle of Salamis. Arrows, stones and spears rained between the ships, but the Greeks' key weapon was the ramming power of their galleys, driven at speed by banks of rowers.

△ *Greek foot soldiers were called hoplites. A man had to buy his own armour, made of bronze. On the march, a slave would carry the heavy armour for his master.*

Phalanx

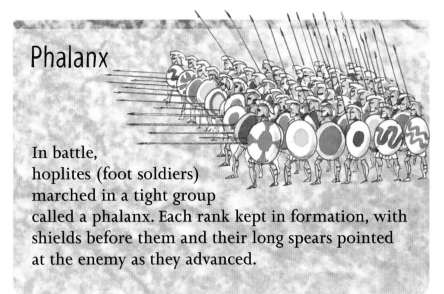

In battle, hoplites (foot soldiers) marched in a tight group called a phalanx. Each rank kept in formation, with shields before them and their long spears pointed at the enemy as they advanced.

Athens had the best navy in Greece. Sparta had the best army. Sparta's economy, like that of Athens, was based on slave workers. There was no democracy. Sport was encouraged, and girls as well as boys were expected to be fit and athletic. Sparta was like an army camp, in which everyone was expected to obey. Boys as young as seven were taken from home and trained to be soldiers.

War with Persia

Only fear of foreign invasion made Athens and Sparta fight side by side, as they did to drive off the Persians. First Darius of Persia, and then his son Xerxes, tried to conquer Greece.

The Greeks fought desperately, at Marathon and at Thermopylae, where a small Spartan rearguard held off the Persian army. The naval victory at Salamis and the land battle of Plataea saved Greece from becoming part of the Persian Empire.

Under Pericles, Athens enjoyed a 'Golden Age'. The city was rebuilt, and the Parthenon temple was erected on the Acropolis. But still Athens and Sparta could not live together in peace. A war between them, called the Peloponnesian War, lasted 27 years. Athens was brought to its knees, and was never the same again.

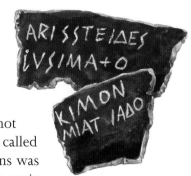

△ *Broken pieces of pottery were used for letter-writing in the Greek world. Clay fragments are still found today, with business notes written on them.*

"Herodotus... here displays his inquiry so that great and marvellous deeds – some displayed by Greeks, some by barbarians – may not be without their glory."

THE HISTORIES, HERODOTUS (c. 485-45 BC)

Herodotus aimed to record the causes of these wars, as well as the wars themselves.

BC

In many ways, ancient Greece was the birthplace of Western civilization. In the small Greek cities, and especially in Athens, people gathered to discuss new ideas. The word 'philosophy' comes from two Greek words meaning love of wisdom, and it is to the Greeks that we owe many of our ideas about beauty, justice and government.

Greek Art and Science

First record of Olympic Games.	776 BC
Iliad and Odyssey stories first collected.	700 BC
Start of Athens' Golden Age.	477 BC
The Parthenon in Athens is completed.	432 BC
Birth of the philosopher Plato.	429 BC
Writings of Herodotus, called the 'Father of History'.	400s BC
Death of Socrates.	399 BC
Birth of philosopher and scientist Aristotle.	384 BC

The Greeks were never united as one nation, but they shared the same language and religion, and many similar ideas about the world.

Science and philosophy

The ancient Greeks were pioneers in medicine, mathematics and science. They looked at the world in the light of logic and reason, and made some fundamental discoveries. In the 400s BC Democritus declared that

△ In a Greek theatre the actors performed on a flat platform called the orchestra. Audiences sat in the open air, on a hillside, although there were seats and some people brought their own cushions. Audiences might watch four plays in a single day.

everything was made of atoms. Aristarchus of Samos (200s BC) knew the Earth was round, and even suggested that it travelled around the Sun.

The names of great Greek scientists such as Archimedes are familiar to this day. Socrates, Plato and Aristotle were three of the greatest philosophers of that, or any other, age. But the common people were often suspicious of their questioning and free thinking. Socrates was sentenced to death in 399 BC for his views.

The gods

The Greeks believed in many gods. Each city had its own protector god or goddess, and families made offerings to household gods too. The gods were thought to live on Mount Olympus, under the rule of Zeus, the king of the gods. Greek gods were immortal, but they had human characteristics too – such as displaying love and jealousy.

Art and literature

The Greeks built many beautiful temples to their gods. They developed an elegant architecture based on mathematical rules, and the use of three styles for the stone columns that are a feature of many Greek buildings.

Greek sculptors portrayed the human body in superb lifelike detail. Music also flourished, often to accompany dances or stories. The most famous stories were the heroic tales of Homer, but the Greeks also invented theatre as we know it, and some of their plays are still performed, in many languages other than Greek.

△ *The Parthenon in Athens was built to honour the city's protector, the goddess Athene. Her gold and ivory decorated statue was inside the great hall, enclosed by columns which supported the roof like a forest of stone trees.*

△ *Greek actors wore masks to show what kind of character (comic or tragic) they played. The finest play-writers were the Athenian dramatists Aeschylus, Sophocles, Euripides (who wrote tragedies) and Aristophanes (who wrote comedies).*

Olympic Games

The Olympic Games are first recorded in 776 BC. People from all over Greece came to take part in or watch the Games, held every four years at Olympia. Sports such as running and discus throwing were to honour Zeus. The winners received crowns of olive leaves.

The Greek way of life spread around the Mediterranean, as traders and colonists settled in new places. The Greeks were scornful of foreigners, calling them 'barbarians'. Yet Greek culture could be found across southern Europe and North Africa, far away from Greece itself.

Daily Life and Trade in Greece

Greeks begin to settle in colonies outside Greece.	750 BC
Colonists found city-states in Sicily, Crete, Cyprus and along the coast of Africa.	750–600 BC
Greek colonists establish the city of Massilia (modern Marseilles).	c. 600 BC
Greeks begin to use coins minted from silver.	500 BC
Classical period of Greek civilization.	500–336 BC
The Peloponnesian War between Athens and Sparta.	431–404 BC
Macedonians defeat the Greeks.	338 BC

Greek homes were built around a central courtyard, cool and airy, where the family slaves prepared food on an open fire, and there was a small shrine to the household god. Many houses were made without windows in the outer walls. This design kept out both the hot sun and thieves.

Business in the town

Greek towns were a centre for government, religion and trade. In the town's marketplace, farmers sold produce such as cheese, wheat, meat, eggs, sheepskins and olive oil. Fast-food sellers did a brisk lunchtime trade in sausages and pancakes. In the dusty lanes around the marketplace, skilled

△ In a Greek country house, the family relaxed in a shady courtyard during the heat of the day. People ate with their fingers, lying on wooden couches, as slaves brought in the dishes and a musician played on pipes or the lyre. Men and women wore a chiton, a cloth square draped over the body and fastened by a pin at the shoulder.

△ *Much of what we know about how the Greeks lived comes from pictures on vases. The pictures show wars and stories from mythology, but also daily activities such as hunting, farming and fishing.*

Cargo ships

Greek ships were wooden, with one square sail. Cargo ships were rounder and slower than war galleys, and often had no oars. In ships with no deck, skins or cloths covered the cargo.

craftworkers carried on their businesses. They included sandal-makers, potters, tanners (who prepared animal skins), armourers, blacksmiths and jewellers.

Farming and fishing

Wherever they settled, Greek farmers relied on three main crops: grapes, olives and grain. Oxen pulled wooden ploughs, but much of the work of sowing and harvesting was done by hand. Grapes were made into wine. Wine and olive oil were stored in large two-handled jars called amphoras. Olive oil was used for cooking, as a fuel in lamps and for washing (the Greeks did not use soap).

Most colonies were near the sea, fishermen sold freshly caught fish in the market. Greek colonists enjoyed stories about sea creatures, sea gods, and the heroic legends of 'the old country' – the peninsula of mainland Greece.

Traders

Greek traders sailed into the Black Sea and along the coast of North Africa. Merchant ships probably went beyond the Mediterranean, as far north as Britain. Trade with the 'barbarians' (people who spoke no Greek) was done by silent exchange of goods, more being offered until both parties were happy with the deal.

"Thucydides the Athenian wrote the history of the war fought between Athens and Sparta in the belief that it was going to be a great war.

HISTORY OF THE PELOPONNESIAN WAR, THUCYDIDES

The Greek historian Thucydides fought in the Peloponnesian War before writing his history."

△ *A portrait of a Greek woman on a fragment of pottery. Greek women spent most of their time around the home, organizing the household and supervising the family's slaves.*

One man took the Greek world into a new age, looking east towards Asia. He was Alexander of Macedonia, known to history as Alexander the Great.

Alexander the Great

Alexander was the son of the soldier-king Philip of Macedon and Olympias, princess of Epirus. Philip's power had grown while Athens and Sparta were at war. He made his small northern kingdom a power to be feared. The Macedonian army joined with the Greeks in 338 BC to defeat the Persians.

The victory against the Persians brought unity, but in Philip's moment of triumph he was cut down by an assassin. His son Alexander, only 20, became king. Alexander had been taught by the wise scholar Aristotle, and had shown a love for learning. But his greatest gift was ruthless generalship. His first act was to crush a revolt by the people of Thebes, to secure his grip on Greece.

Alexander's campaigns

In just 13 years, Alexander led his army out of Europe and into Asia. He started off with 35,000 men. First, he crushed the might of Persia and swept through Syria into Egypt. There he was welcomed as a liberator from Persian rule. He founded the city of Alexandria, which became one of the great cities of learning and trade of the ancient world.

From Egypt, Alexander marched into Mesopotamia and Babylonia. The Persians had regrouped, but he defeated their army at Gaugamela. Alexander burned the

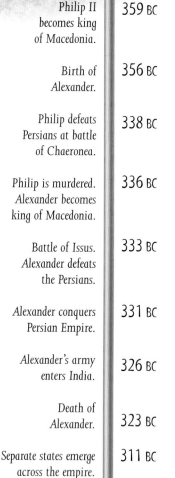

Philip II becomes king of Macedonia.	359 BC
Birth of Alexander.	356 BC
Philip defeats Persians at battle of Chaeronea.	338 BC
Philip is murdered. Alexander becomes king of Macedonia.	336 BC
Battle of Issus. Alexander defeats the Persians.	333 BC
Alexander conquers Persian Empire.	331 BC
Alexander's army enters India.	326 BC
Death of Alexander.	323 BC
Separate states emerge across the empire.	311 BC

▷ On his horse Bucephalus, Alexander leads his troops into battle at Issus in 333 BC. The horse was said to be too spirited and wild until tamed by Alexander.

△ *Alexander, shown here, believed that the Greek hero Achilles was his ancestor. He learned by heart the account of Achilles' deeds in the epic poem, the Iliad.*

Alexandria

The city of Alexandria in Egypt was founded in 332 BC. It became famous for its library, established in the 200s BC by the Egyptian kings Ptolemy I and Ptolemy II. Its lighthouse was one of the Seven Wonders of the Ancient World.

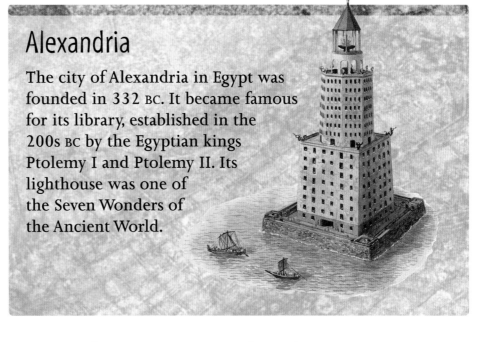

△ *Alexander imposed a single system of money throughout his lands. He was keen to promote trade and commerce across the empire too.*

Persian city of Persepolis, and shortly afterwards the Persian king Darius was killed by his own side.

Afghanistan and India

This astonishing campaign took Alexander's army eastwards, into Afghanistan, and as far north as Tashkent in central Asia, before he turned south towards India. In 326 BC Alexander entered what is now Pakistan and defeated the Indian king Porus. He hoped to find the mythical river Ocean, which encircled the world, but his troops would go no farther. They endured a terrible return journey across the desert of Gedrosia.

The world empire

Alexander decided to make Babylon the capital of his new 'world empire'. He married a Persian princess and hired soldiers of all nationalities. Everywhere he went, Greek ideas went too. Alexander was planning new conquests when he became ill and died in Babylon, just before his 33rd birthday.

Without Alexander's genius, his empire soon broke up into smaller states ruled by his generals. The strongest of these were Macedonia, Egypt and the Asian kingdom of Seleucus Nicator.

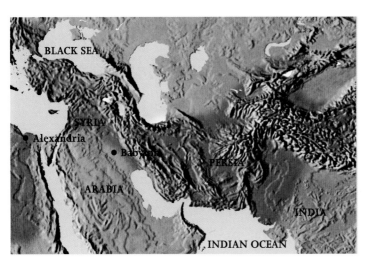

◁ *Alexander's empire stretched from Greece to North Africa and as far east as India and Afghanistan. He ruled most of what was then thought of as 'the civilized world'. After his death, Alexander was buried in the city of Alexandria.*

71

BC

By about 600 BC India was a jigsaw puzzle of kingdoms and tribal states. In the state of Kapilavastu, Gautama Buddha, founder of one of the world's great religions, was born in about 566 BC.

New Indian Empires

Most people in India at that time followed the ancient religious beliefs of Hinduism. However, the teachings of Buddha found favour with powerful rulers and Buddhism spread quickly in India.

The rise of Chandragupta

By the 400s BC the most powerful state in India was the kingdom of Magadha, which had its capital at Patna. Yet its control was weakening. It is said that while Alexander the Great was marching into India in 325 BC, he met a young Indian ruler named Chandragupta Maurya. Chandragupta also had ambition. He seized the throne of Magadha and

Birth of Buddha.	566 BC
Chandragupta rules small kingdom of Nanda.	321 BC
Alexander the Great invades India.	326 BC
Chandragupta wins control of Greek-held lands in India and Afghanistan.	303 BC
Bindusara succeeds his father Chandragupta.	297 BC
Asoka Maurya becomes emperor.	272 BC
Asoka conquers Kalinga (Orissa) and becomes a Buddhist.	261 BC
Death of Asoka.	232 BC

△ A detail of stone carving on the Buddhist stupa at Sanchi in India, dating from the 100s BC. It shows a parade with musicians and a ruler being driven in a two-horse chariot.

△ Buddhism is still one of the world's foremost religions, with devotees all over the modern world.

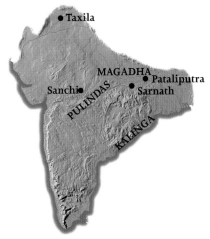

△ The extent of the Mauryan Empire during the reign of Asoka. He extended the limits of the empire until most of India was under Mauryan rule.

△ The carved stone lions on the pillar at Sarnath have become a national emblem for India.

Asoka

Asoka was probably the greatest ruler of ancient India. He became a vegetarian after adopting Buddhism, and tried to follow Buddha's teachings of non-violence. After years of soldiering and killing, Asoka believed that everyone should respect all living things. He travelled in his empire, hearing the ideas and problems of his subjects.

took advantage of the upheaval caused by Alexander's campaigns to seize a large chunk of territory in the north.

The Mauryan Empire

So began the Mauryan Empire. Chandragupta's son Bindusara continued and extended his conquests. The old capital of Patna (then called Pataliputra) was now the centre of an empire that stretched from the Arabian Sea in the west to the Bay of Bengal in the east. Only the southern tip of the Indian subcontinent lay outside its territory.

Emperor Asoka

Chandragupta's grandson Asoka was the greatest emperor of ancient India. He took government very seriously, reforming taxes, encouraging trade and farming, and building walled cities with pleasant houses and paved streets. His officials travelled the country, building roads (including what Indians now know as the Great Trunk Road) and collecting taxes from peasant farmers in villages.

Asoka was born a Hindu, but he became a Buddhist. He then gave up war, sickened by the slaughter he had seen during his conquest of Orissa in the southeast. He urged his people to be tolerant of others and to respect all life.

Asoka's laws

Asoka made new laws and had them inscribed on stone pillars set up all across his empire. There are ten still standing today, the most famous at Sarnath near the Hindu holy city of Benares (Varanasi). The tall pillar at Sarnath is topped with four carved lions and four wheels. The wheel, often referred to as the 'wheel of life', is an important symbol of Buddhism.

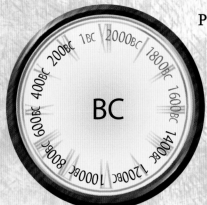

BC

Peoples all over the world formed systems of beliefs in powers greater than their own. The earliest religions were connected with the forces of nature – the Sun, the Moon, wind, water, rocks and trees – and with animals.

Eastern Religions

The great religions of the world all began in Asia. Three of them – Judaism, Christianity and Islam – began in the same area of west Asia. Hinduism and Buddhism began in India.

In the civilizations of the ancient world the king was often seen as the gods' representative. The god-king defended his people. The Egyptians believed in many gods, and in a life after death. One pharaoh, Akhenaton, tried to replace the old gods with a 'one-god' faith based on sun worship. The experiment was short-lived.

Rig Vedas, earliest Hindu holy songs, written in India.	1500 BC
Jews leave Egypt (the Exodus). Moses receives the Ten Commandments.	1200 BC
Hindu Upanishads, or holy books, name a supreme spirit called Brahman.	700 BC
Zarathrustra (Zoroaster) in Persia.	c. 600s BC
The scholar Confucius teaches in China.	500s BC
Lao-tzu writes the Tao Te Ching, about the unity of all things in nature.	500s BC
Jainism, in India, founded by a wise man named Mahavira.	500 BC
Buddhism spreads in India after Asoka becomes a Buddhist.	200s BC

△ Buddhism was taught by a prince named Gautama Buddha. In this picture he is shown meditating under a shady bodhi tree in an Indian village.

△ *Hindu pilgrims came to bathe in the waters of the holy river Ganges, as people still do today.*

India

Hinduism is the oldest of the Asian beliefs. There are many Hindu gods, and rules governing foods, behaviour, festivals and even which jobs people may do.

Buddhism began in India in the 500s BC, and was later spread by missionaries to Burma and China. In its birthplace of India, Buddhism practically died out. It was different from other religions in having no god or gods. Its followers were taught to escape the sufferings of life by desiring nothing. Another Indian religion, Jainism, forbade its followers to kill any living thing, even an insect.

Judaism

The Jews were the first people in Europe and Asia to put their faith in one god. They believed that they were a chosen people, who owed their escape from slavery in Egypt and Babylon to a supreme God whom they called Yahweh (the Lord). God gave the Ten Commandments (laws) to Moses, and prophets delivered messages from God. Jews believed that God would send a messiah, or saviour, to bring justice and peace. Later, followers of Jesus Christ, a Jew, believed he was the Messiah (the Son of God).

△ *Hindu sculptures of gods and goddesses are full of energy. The four-armed Vishnu is the preserver of the Universe. He is one of Hinduism's two main gods – the other is Shiva.*

Confucius

In China, people worshipped their ancestors and nature spirits. In the 500s BC, a scholar named Confucius taught a system of 'right behaviour' which has influenced Chinese government and society ever since. He taught loyalty to the family, worship of ancestors, and obedience to the laws of society.

△ *A bronze statue of Buddha. The name Buddha means 'the enlightened one'.*

The first emperor of China, Shih Huang-di, created enormous upheaval. The building of the Great Wall was just one sign of this upheaval, for the emperor was a ruthless tyrant. Millions of poor Chinese were forced to work as labourers on the Great Wall and other vast building projects.

Han Rule in China

End of the Qin dynasty.	206 BC
Liu Pang becomes the first Han emperor.	202 BC
Start of Wu-ti's reign. Wars against the Hun.	140 BC
Wang Mang becomes emperor, briefly founding the Hsin dynasty.	AD 9
Huns raid China and burn Chang-an.	AD 23
Han dynasty restored by emperor Liu Hsiu.	AD 25
Buddhism has reached China by this time.	AD 100
Han power begins to decline.	AD 125
End of the Han dynasty.	AD 220

Only four years after the emperor's death, the army and the mass of peasants were up in arms. From this rebellion emerged a new dynasty, the Han. The first Han emperor was Liu Pang, a minor official turned soldier, whose parents had been peasants themselves.

The Han emperors

The Han rulers made the city of Chang-an their capital. It was defended by thick walls, 18 metres high in places. The emperor lived in a magnificent palace, among his wives, concubines, courtiers and guards.

Chinese rulers were superstitious, employing court magicians and fortune-tellers. During the period of Han rule, large stone statues were placed outside tombs. There were also enormous figures of Buddha, for Buddhism reached China in the first century AD.

Most ordinary people lived in one-room shacks, and were very poor. Merchants were not allowed to live within the city walls. They were considered inferior to wheat farmers or women who reared silkworms.

China's trade links

It was during the Han dynasty that Chinese traders first had regular

△ A bustling street in the Chinese city of Chang-an (modern Xian). Traders regulated by city officials sold everything from livestock to jewellery. Scribes, artists and craftworkers were kept busy in what was, in the 100s BC, probably the world's biggest city.

△ These soldiers are part of the huge army of terracotta figures buried near the tomb of the first Chinese emperor, Shi Huang-di. As well as thousands of warriors, the burial army also included clay horses and chariots. The figures were placed in three pits inside the large complex surrounding the emperor's tomb.

The Silk Road

The Silk Road stretched 4,000 kilometres across central Asia. Chinese traders travelled along this route, bringing their brightly coloured silks to sell to merchants in the ports and cities of Europe.

contact with the West, and with an empire as large as China's — Rome. From Chang-an, traders followed the Silk Road, crossing the smaller empires of Kushan and Parthia to reach the Mediterranean shores and the Roman world. Chinese silk fetched a high price, for the secret of making silk was unknown in the West.

Attacks from the Huns

Fearing attack from the Hsiung Nu or Hun, fierce horsemen from the north, the Chinese at first tried to buy them off with bribes. Under the strong Han emperor, Wu-ti (149–87 BC), the Hun came back to attack the Chinese capital of Chang-an, and there was savage fighting.

Wu-ti sent his armies west into central Asia to punish the Huns. While there, the Chinese reinforced their defences. They rounded up large, fast horses for their cavalry. They added new stretches to the Great Wall to keep out the Huns. But over the years the Huns' repeated attacks weakened China. In AD 23, the nomads poured into China again and burned Chang-an. Han emperors reigned until AD 220, but their power was weakened. After Han rule ended, China, without a unifying ruler, split into several smaller kingdoms.

Green is the grass on the riverbanks/ Dense are the willows in the garden/ Fair is the woman upstairs/ Bright as the moon at her window.

ANONYMOUS HAN DYNASTY POEM c. AD 100

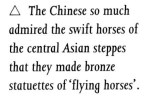

△ The Chinese so much admired the swift horses of the central Asian steppes that they made bronze statuettes of 'flying horses'.

BC/AD

People from mainland Asia had settled on the islands of Japan by 7000 BC. The original inhabitants may have been the Ainu, about 15,000 of whom still live in Japan.

Japan

The early Japanese lived by hunting and fishing. Farming began around 1000 to 500 BC, when the Japanese learned to grow rice, a skill learned from China. They also began to make metal tools and to make pottery using a potter's wheel. The site in Tokyo where pottery from this time was first found gives this period of Japanese history its name: Yayoi.

Rice farming begins in Japan.	1000 BC
Traditional date of Japan's first emperor, Jimmu Tenno.	660 BC
Start of the Yayoi period. Bronze and iron tools.	250 BC
Chinese visit Japan and report on its way of life.	AD 240
Growth of Yamato power in Japan.	AD 300
Japan probably unified under one ruler around this time.	AD 350
New ideas are brought from China. Japan rules part of Korea.	AD 400s
Yamato power declines. Japan loses its grip on Korea.	AD 500s

Village life
The Yayoi farmers dug ditches to irrigate their rice fields. They built thatched homes and storehouses on stilts for their rice crop. Farmers lived together in villages, and each village was led by a chief who was often a woman shaman, or magician. The women shamans of Japan were powerful figures. In the 200s BC a shaman named Himiko used her authority to end a civil war between numerous small states. According to legend, Japan had its first emperor in the 600s BC but there is no historical evidence of his existence.

Contact with China
About AD 240, the Chinese sent ambassadors to the islands of Japan. These visitors wrote reports on what they saw,

▷ *A typical Yayoi farming scene, showing their thatched homes and storehouses on stilts, and the ditches to irrigate their rice fields.*

▷ The Chinese sent ships to report on what was going on in Japan. They called Japan 'Wo', and regarded it as a subject country. Relations between the two countries seem to have been friendly, since Japan posed no threat to China.

△ A modern Ainu elder in traditional dress. A few Ainu people still live in separate village communities, following their traditional way of life, but most have integrated into modern Japanese society.

giving historians the first detailed view of life in Japan at this time. The Chinese saw large towns and cemeteries - the Japanese buried their dead in large pottery jars or in stone coffins. The Japanese admired the Chinese and copied the way the Chinese wrote, the Chinese calendar and the teachings of the scholar Confucius.

Warlords and emperors

By the AD 300s the Japanese had become expert in making iron tools and weapons. Shaman chiefs still ruled the villages, but there were now powerful warlords who led bands of warriors. These warrior-bands or clans (related families) fought for power.

Warlords were buried in huge tombs, beneath earth mounds, some of which were shaped like keyholes. The body of the dead ruler was laid to rest dressed in armour, with his weapons beside him, and with rich gold and jade jewellery.

By AD 400 one clan, the Yamato, had become supreme. They controlled central Japan and parts of southern Korea. The Yamato chiefs were the first real emperors, and are regarded as the ancestors of Japan's present royal family.

Burying the dead

During Japan's Yayoi period, from 250 BC the dead were often buried inside wooden coffins or stone tombs. Stones were used to mark out the area of a burial site. Sometimes burial rites involved placing the body inside a double jar made of pottery, such as the one shown here. The tallest of these Japanese burial jars was more than two metres high.

△ The Yayoi people made bell-shaped objects called dotaku out of bronze. They were decorated with pictures of animals or scenes from daily life.

BC

The Celts came from central Europe, although their previous origins are unclear. Around 500 BC, perhaps to escape wars with their Germanic neighbours, they began to move westwards. Groups of people settled in what are now Spain, France, Britain and Ireland.

Celtic Europe

Evidence of Celts in Austria, from graves.	700 BC
Celts spread westwards across Europe, and also to the south and east.	500 BC
Celts attack and loot Rome.	390 BC
Romans counterattack and invade Cisalpine Gaul in northern Italy.	192 BC
Gauls and Romans fight for control of Massilia (Marseilles) in France.	100s BC
The Belgae, a Celtic tribe, move across the English Channel to settle in Britain.	75 BC
Julius Caesar tries to invade Celtic Britain, but withdraws.	55 BC
Caesar invades Britiain again. Celts agree to pay tribute (tax) to Rome.	54 BC

Some Celts, known to the Romans as Gauls, invaded Italy and others went as far east as Greece and Asia Minor. The Celts were warlike and their arrival usually led to fighting. In the British Isles, Celtic invaders sometimes drove out the local Britons, but elsewhere settled peacefully alongside them. They brought with them their languages, which became the Welsh and Gaelic still spoken more than 2,000 years later.

Warriors in hillforts

Celtic warriors fought in horse-drawn chariots and on foot, often with wild bravery. They were quarrelsome and often fought among themselves. But they were also skilled in farming and using iron to make tools and weapons.

To protect themselves and their farm animals, the Celts built forts on hilltops. Large family groups lived in or around these hillforts, taking shelter inside if attacked. The hillforts were oval or round, with earth ramparts topped by wooden stockades. The biggest, such as Maiden Castle in Dorset, had two or more ramparts and gateways defended by walls that curved out like horns, giving defenders a clear shot at anyone trying to break down the gate.

△ *A Celtic hillfort was surrounded by a ditch and an earth rampart topped by a wooden stockade. The round houses inside had conical thatched roofs and walls made of woven sticks plastered over with mud. The settlement's gateway was well defended against attack.*

△ *Around the campfire at night, Celtic poets, storytellers and musicians would pass on tales of the gods and of events in the history of the Celtic people.*

Druids

Celtic priests called druids performed mysterious rites in sacred groves of trees. The Moon, the oak tree and mistletoe were all magical to the Celts, and so too were many animals.

Art and legend

The Celts were artistic people. They loved stories and music, and they made beautiful jewellery and metalwork decorated with abstract designs and animal shapes.

They had no written language, passing on their legends of gods and heroes in stories around the fire. Most of what we know of the Celts comes from the writings of their enemies, such as the Romans. The Celts themselves left a legacy of art and legend, and language – Welsh, Breton, Cornish, Irish and Scottish Gaelic are all Celtic languages.

Loyalty and sacrifice

The Celts were led by chiefs. Each warrior swore loyalty to his chief, who rewarded his followers with feasting and booty after victory. The various tribes never came together in a lasting state.

The Celts believed in many gods, some of whom were rather unattractive, such as pot-bellied Dagda, whose club could deliver either life or death. Celtic religion involved human sacrifice, although most reports of bloodthirsty practices come from the Romans, who thought the Celts were brave but barbarous.

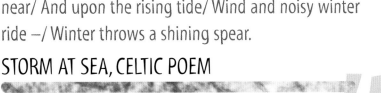

Tempest on the plain of Lir/ Bursts its barriers far and near/ And upon the rising tide/ Wind and noisy winter ride –/ Winter throws a shining spear.

STORM AT SEA, CELTIC POEM

△ *The Celts were expert metalworkers, making fine objects out of gold, silver and bronze. Their work featured geometric designs, animals and human faces.*

BC

Rome grew from a small kingdom in Italy. It became a republic and one of the mightiest empires of the ancient world, with an empire stretching the length of the Mediterranean Sea.

The Rise of Rome

According to tradition, the city of Rome was founded in 753 BC. Legends say that early Rome was ruled by Etruscan kings, of whom Romulus was the first. Romulus and his twin brother Remus were suckled by a she-wolf after being abandoned by their wicked great-uncle. They founded Rome, but the brothers quarrelled and Remus was killed.

Traditional date for founding of Rome.	753 BC
Roman Republic founded after overthrow of King Tarquinius Superbus.	510 BC
Plebeians (workers) revolt against patricians (aristocrats).	494 BC
Work starts on the Appian Way.	312 BC
Rome defeats Gauls, Samnites and Latins in Third Samnite War.	298 BC
Patricians and plebeians share equal rights in Rome.	287 BC
Start of Punic Wars between Rome and Carthage.	264 BC
Carthaginian general Hannibal crosses Alps to attack Italy.	218 BC

The Etruscans, who came from Etruria in northern Italy, chose a strong position for their city on the top of seven hills. To the south lived the Latini, or Latins. In time both peoples became simply Romans.

The republic

In about 510 BC, the Etruscan kings were driven out of Rome, which became a republic. The Roman Republic was ruled by the Senate, which consisted of a group of elders who elected two consuls each year to lead them. The senators advised the consuls, but the consuls were powerful in their own right.

The typical Roman citizen was a peasant with a small farm. About 200 BC large estates owned by townspeople began to grow up, using slave labour.

△ A busy street in ancient Rome. Some buildings had several storeys, and citizens collected water from a communal trough. Roman shops opened onto the street. Wine and oil sellers, butchers and bakers did good business, and at times laws were passed to stop traders cluttering up the pavements.

△ Etruscan warriors. The Etruscans, the masters of central Italy in the 500s BC, were defeated by the Romans.

Roman Villa

A Roman villa was a large comfortable country home, with hot-air central heating and a courtyard for fine weather. The family had servants to run the house and slaves to work on the farm.

The power of the army

Rome rose to power thanks to its fertile farmland, its army and its key position in the middle of Italy. One of its earliest roads, the Appian Way, was built in 312 BC so that soldiers could travel southwards. The Roman army was the best in Europe. By 200 BC Rome was Italy's leading power. It was able to challenge and defeat rivals such as Carthage for control of the Mediterranean world.

Everyday life in town and country

The Romans believed town and countryside should be organized and peaceful. They built walls around their towns for protection. Within the walls were shops and houses, both large and small. There were blocks of flats too. Rich and poor went to the public baths to wash, relax and meet friends. Every town had its temples dedicated to protector gods and goddesses. Business was done in the forum, originally the town marketplace.

In the countryside, Romans lived with their servants in villas on big estates. Some villas were run as large farms. The owners kept sheep and cows, and vineyards were also profitable. The owner and his family lived in a comfortable house with its own garden.

He succeeded in founding his city, and installing the gods of his race in the Latin land... that was the origin of the Latin nation and the proud battlements of Rome.

THE AENEID, VIRGIL (70-19 BC)

Virgil was a Roman poet. He wrote his poem The Aeneid *to tell the mythical history of the founding of Rome by the poem's hero, Aeneas.*

△ Part of a carved stone relief depicting a Roman funeral procession. The pallbearers carry the dead person on a raised bier, followed by the mourners.

BC/AD

Having destroyed the power of Carthage in 201 BC, the Romans began to build an empire. The Celts, the Seleucid kings, the Greeks and the Egyptians all fell before Roman power. Only the Parthians in the east and the Germanic tribes in northwest Europe defied the mighty Roman army.

The Roman Empire

Rome was a republic, with a form of democracy, but strong leaders were ambitious for sole power. In 49 BC Julius Caesar (100–44 BC) attacked Gaul. Like all successful Roman leaders, he knew that victory would bring booty, captives and cheers from the people in Rome.

In 44 BC Caesar was murdered by plotters who feared he might become king. Civil war broke out. After the war Caesar's great-nephew Octavius, thereafter known as Augustus, became Rome's first emperor.

The empire
At its peak, the Roman Empire stretched from Britain in the west to Mesopotamia in the east. The army defended this empire. As well as fighting, Roman soldiers built roads, forts and aqueducts. They guarded the borders while Roman ships patrolled the Mediterranean trade routes. A network of roads criss-crossed the empire, linking towns and forts.

Roman peace
Most people accepted Roman rule for the benefits it brought, letting them farm and trade in peace.

After conquering Gaul, Julius Caesar invades Britain.	55 BC
Caesar is murdered.	44 BC
Romans conquer Egypt. Cleopatra and Mark Antony are defeated.	31 BC
Octavius becomes emperor, and calls himself Augustus.	27 BC
Romans invade Britain.	AD 43
Volcanic eruption buries town of Pompeii in Italy.	AD 79
Roman Empire at its greatest.	AD 100
Barbarian attacks on Roman Empire increase.	AD 180
Visigoths attack Rome.	AD 410

▷ Gladiators were trained to fight in the arena. Some carried a shield and sword, others fought with a net and a long three-pronged spear, or trident.

84

▷ *The Circus Maximus in Rome was packed with fans of chariot racing. Races were fast and furious, with frequent violent crashes, and winning drivers became rich superstars.*

△ *Part of the complex of Roman baths in the city of Bath, in England. Romans would visit the public baths to bathe in hot and cold pools, and also to relax and talk with their friends.*

Towns grew, even in remote corners of the empire such as Britain. Wherever they went, the Romans built towns with baths, temples and theatres, and in the countryside comfortable farmhouses called villas, many of which even had central heating.

To keep the mass of the people amused, Roman rulers presided over religious holidays, victory parades, and games in the arenas where mock battles and fights between gladiators were staged before vast, noisy crowds. Chariot racing was also popular, with heavy betting on races.

The Roman way

People throughout the Empire adopted Roman ways. Latin was widely used as the language of government, along with Greek, the language of scholars. Many people took to wearing Roman clothes, and thought of themselves as Romans.

The Romans were great borrowers – they adopted many gods from other cultures and they copied Greek styles in architecture and art. But they were also inventors. The Romans were the first to make concrete, and they used the arch to make roofs that spanned large inside spaces, without the need for columns.

A vast empire

Rome benefited greatly from its position in the middle of Italy. Through their economic power and by winning wars against their neighbours, the Romans were able to create one of the largest empires in history.

△ *Slaves made up about a third of Rome's population. At the slave auctions, slaves wore tags advertising their skills and good character.*

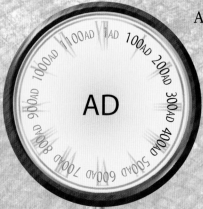

AD

At this time the Roman Empire was governed by the personal will of the emperor, but the emperor's power rested on the army. Weak or bad emperors were sometimes overthrown by army generals. Some emperors ruled well – Hadrian, for example, travelled widely to inspect building projects. Others, such as Nero and Caligula, were cruel or mad.

War and Government

Caligula is emperor.	AD 37–51
Claudius is emperor.	AD 41–54
Romans invade Britain.	AD 43
Colchester becomes a 'colony' for retired Roman soldiers.	AD 49
Nero is emperor. Rome burns.	AD 54–68
Birth of Tacitus, a Roman historian who wrote about the conquest of Britain.	AD 56
Boudicca leads a revolt against the Romans in Britain.	AD 60
Vespasian, a former soldier in Britain, is emperor.	AD 68–79
Trajan is emperor. There are 31 legions, the highest number yet.	AD 98–117
Hadrian is emperor.	AD 117–138
The empire is divided.	AD 395
Rome is captured and burned by the Visigoths.	AD 410

The Romans were such good organizers that the empire usually kept working even when there was a fool at its centre. It was divided into provinces, such as Britannia (Britain), each ruled by a governor or legate (chosen person). The governor had a staff of officials, who looked after finance, army matters, law-making, trade and all the other affairs of government.

The legions

The Roman army's main fighting troops were its legions. Each legion had up to 5,000 men, whose training and discipline were usually a match for any enemies they faced.

A legionary soldier wore armour to protect his body. On the road he marched at a steady pace, carrying his kit hung on a pole over one shoulder. He carried clothes, a food dish, cooking pot, rations and tools.

▷ Most Roman soldiers fought on foot, although cavalry were used for patrols and in battle. Cavalrymen were sometimes recruited from foreign countries.

▷ Emperor Trajan (ruled AD 91–117) built a monument 30 metres high to the Roman army. Its carved reliefs show soldiers doing all kinds of tasks, from storming a fort to building a camp. This section shows Roman legionaries, who were builders as well as fighters, constructing a fort.

△ Octavian, a great-nephew of Julius Caesar, took the title Augustus as first emperor (27 BC to AD 14). The month of August was named in his honour.

Taking control

As soon as a new province was conquered, the army set up bases to control it. In Britain, the Romans invaded in AD 43, and having defeated the southern tribes, began building forts and roads.

When the eastern Britons rose in revolt under Queen Boudicca, the Romans were at first defeated, then regrouped and won a decisive victory. The Romans took revenge, burning farms and villages, but soon saw this was a mistake. They changed to 'Romanizing' – making conquered Britain prosperous so that its people would no longer want to fight Rome. By AD 100, the Romans controlled England and Wales as far north as Hadrian's Wall in northern England.

Rome's power weakens

In the end, not even the Roman army could control such a huge empire. From AD 200 the army was stretched to defend the frontiers, especially in the east (Balkans) and northwest (Germany). Barbarian attacks increased. Britain was abandoned in the early 400s, soon after the empire had split into eastern and western halves. The western half crumbled, leaving the Eastern Empire, at Constantinople (now Istanbul Turkey), to preserve the legacy of Rome into a new age.

Hadrian's Wall

Hadrian's Wall was built in AD 122 to defend the northern frontier of Roman Britain. It acted as a checkpoint on movement between England and Scotland. The wall took eight years to build and stretches for 118 km.

△ A Roman coin stamped with the head of the Emperor Hadrian. During his reign, he personally visited nearly every province in the Roman Empire.

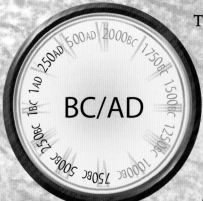

BC/AD

The Greeks believed in many different gods, chief among these were a family of supernatural beings who lived on Mount Olympus and watched over humanity. Certain gods looked after the harvest; others cared for wild animals, the sea, war and so on. The Romans took over many of these Greek gods and gave them Latin names.

Ancient Gods

First Olympic Games honour Zeus.	776 BC
Temples on the Acropolis in Athens are built.	400s BC
Socrates is sentenced to death for showing disrespect to the gods.	399 BC
Greece conquered by Rome. Romans adopt many Greek gods and myths.	146 BC
Probable year of Jesus's death. Christianity spreads into the Roman world.	AD 28
Many Romans switch from the old religion to new beliefs.	AD 100s
Persecution of Christians in Rome, during the reign of Diocletian.	AD 200s
Constantine makes Christianity the official religion of the empire.	AD 312

They believed the gods could and did interfere in human affairs, bringing success or disaster. King of the gods was Zeus, whom the Romans called Jupiter. Greeks believed that the Universe was a sphere. The upper half was light and airy, the lower half dark and gloomy. The Earth was a flat disc, floating between the two halves. When people died they went to the Underworld, which was ruled by Hades, the brother of Zeus.

Monsters and heroes

The Greeks also told stories about all kinds of nature spirits – magical beings often half-animal and half-human, such as centaurs (half-human and half-horse). There were fearful monsters that turned people to stone (such as Medusa), but even these horrors could be defeated by heroes, with the help of a friendly god or goddess. Some heroes in Greek myths, such as Odysseus and Jason, even became part of Western culture.

Mars   Minerva

◁ The Romans adopted Greek gods including Minerva (Athena, Greek goddess of wisdom and war). The Roman god Mars was identifed with Ares, the Greek god of war.

▷ A funeral procession passes along a Roman street. The body was carried on a litter for burial, followed by mourners and musicians. Noble Romans in particular honoured their dead ancestors.

△ Ruins of Greek and Roman temples can be seen across Europe, the Near East and North Africa. Every town had its own temple, dedicated to a protector god or goddess.

Gods and god-emperors

The gods of the Greeks and Romans were unpredictable, and too much like humans in many ways. People tried to please the gods by building statues and temples in their honour, and by offering gifts. Each city had its own protector god or gods. Athens was watched over by the goddess Athena. In Rome a huge temple to Jupiter stood on the Capitoline Hill. The gods were honoured by processions and sacrifices, carried out by a priest.

The Romans borrowed gods from all parts of their empire – from Greece, Egypt, Asia Minor, even Celtic Britain. Many soldiers became followers of Mithras, a Persian god. Several emperors were worshipped as gods while still living.

New and old ideas

Most Romans had no clear idea about what happened to people after death, although they were afraid of ghosts, and had a deep respect for ancestors. They were generally tolerant of new beliefs, but the Roman emperors did for a time persecute the new religion of Christianity. By the AD 300s many Romans had adopted the new faith, with its promise of an afterlife in heaven.

Sea god

Poseidon was the Greek god of the sea, and is often shorn carrying a three-pronged spear, called a trident. The Greeks believed Poseidon to be the brother of Zeus, the king of the gods, and Hades, god of the underworld. He was also associated with horses, and the Greeks thought that he was the father of the winged horse, Pegasus.

△ Zeus, king of the Greek gods. The first Olympic Games, which took place in 776 BC, were held in his honour. Zeus was head of a family of gods and goddesses called the Olympians.

The period from AD 500 to AD 1500 in Europe is known as the Middle Ages. It is called 'middle' because it falls between the two worlds of ancient history and modern history, yet the term 'Middle Ages' has no historical meaning in other parts of the world.

The Early Middle Ages

In China, for instance, history is described in terms of dynasties (ruling families), while the history of America is often divided into before Columbus (that is, before the arrival of European settlers) and after.

The world after Rome

Roman rule had created a common cultural framework across much of Europe, North Africa and the Middle East. After the collapse of the Roman Empire, Roman ways continued to influence many people; Roman law, for example, became the basis for much European law. Latin, the language of the Romans, was used by scholars and in government. The Roman Catholic Church used Latin in its services until modern times.

So Roman culture lived on. Historians used to refer to the period after the fall of the Roman Empire as the 'Dark Ages'. Fine cities did fall into ruins, the old Roman roads crumbled, the Roman peace no longer existed. This was a time of movement, uncertainty and violence. Yet it was not all

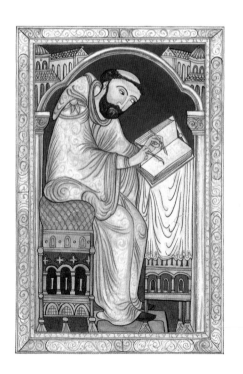

darkness. Great works of art were created, achievements were made in science and architecture, and people performed great feats of heroism and exploration.

The new Europe

Although the Roman Empire in the West had fallen, the Empire in the East held out for a few hundred years. In Europe, the Christian Church was the force that held Europe together. The popes ruled from Rome, like the emperors of old. Christianity spread slowly across Europe, and in monasteries scholar monks preserved many Greek and Roman books for future generations.

A time of change

The early Middle Ages were a time of change. In the Middle East, the new and fast-growing faith of Islam became the backbone of new empires. In Asia, the empires of India and China continued to enjoy a civilization that was more advanced than any in Europe. People were on the move. Arabs and Turks expanded into new lands, Saxons and Angles moved across the North Sea to England. From Scandinavia, the Vikings set out in their longships across the seas to trade, farm and fight.

The period covered by this book ends with the first millennium – and the Norman conquest of England in 1066. This marked a turning-point in the history of Britain, signalling an end to the ancient world. It opened the door to the second half of the Middle Ages, beyond which lay the Renaissance, the Age of Discovery and the dawn of the modern world.

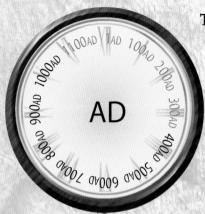

The Roman Empire split in two in AD 395. After the collapse of the western half in AD 476, the eastern part survived. Its capital was Byzantium (now Istanbul in Turkey), a city founded by the Greeks.

The Byzantine Empire

The Roman emperor Constantine gave the city of Byzantium a new name, Constantinople. It became the home of eastern orthodox Christianity, and the capital of the Byzantine emperors.

Byzantium was 'Rome in the East'. Here, artists and scholars carried on the traditions of ancient Greek and Roman culture. The Byzantines loved music, poetry and art, and decorated their churches with beautifully coloured wall paintings, or frescoes, and mosaic pictures. Mosaics are pictures made from small pieces of glass or stone set in patterns.

Wars and laws

The Byzantine Empire was strongest in the AD 500s. The Emperor Justinian had a mighty general, Belisarius, who won many battles. He also had a clever wife, the empress Theodora. Justinian's laws, which gave new rights to women and children, became the framework for later legal systems in many countries in Europe.

△ Chariots raced around the track in the Hippodrome. Entrance was free (the emperors knew that the races kept the mob amused). As well as thrilling and often dangerous races, there were animal fights, dancing girls and circus acts to entertain the huge crowds.

A magnificent city

Most of the people of the Byzantine Empire were farmers. They came to the city to sell goods, and to marvel. Foreigners visiting Constantinople were amazed by its magnificence. Its

Roman Empire divides into East (Byzantium) and West (Rome).	AD 395
Emperor Theodosius repairs and rebuilds the city walls.	AD 408
Fall of the Western Roman Empire.	AD 476
Justinian and Theodora rule Byzantine Empire.	AD 527–565
Byzantines conquer southeastern Spain.	AD 554
Wars with Arabs and religious quarrels weaken Byzantine power.	AD 700s
Byzantine Empire recovers.	AD 900s
Death of Basil II is followed by further period of weak rule.	AD 1025

△ *A 19th-century print of the emperor Justinian and his influential wife Theodora. Through war and diplomacy, Justinian made Byzantium the greatest power in the eastern Mediterranean.*

Eastern empire

The Byzantine Empire swallowed up Turkey, the Balkans, parts of Spain and North Africa, Egypt and the western coasts of the Mediterranean. The Empire was at its height under Justinian.

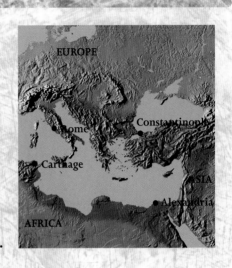

port was packed with ships, its markets swarmed with people of many nations. Richly dressed noblewomen were carried on litters by servants along streets in which slaves and soldiers jostled sailors and merchants.

The city was dominated by the enormous church of Hagia Sophia, to which the emperor and his retinue paraded to celebrate Christian festivals. Built in only six years, between AD 532 and 537, by order of Justininian, the huge domed building is one of the gems of world architecture. Inside the vast Hippodrome, crowds of 60,000 roared with approval or scorn for the chariot racers. Nobles and rich merchants lived in comfortable houses with central heating. Poor families crammed into multi-storey tenement blocks.

As strong as its emperor

The Byzantine empire needed strong rulers. After Justinian's death in AD 565, few rulers came near to matching his power and the empire was weakened by wars. Only vigorous soldiers were able to rally its forces and maintain a grip on its lands and trade.

Byzantium managed to fight off its enemies and survive into the second millennium. Its end came finally in 1453, when the city of Constantinople was captured by the Turks.

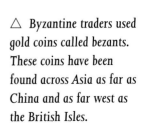

△ *Byzantine traders used gold coins called bezants. These coins have been found across Asia as far as China and as far west as the British Isles.*

Justice is the constant and perpetual wish to render to everyone his due.
EMPEROR JUSTINIAN (c. 482–565)

Most Native Americans were nomads, hunting for food. Yet in North and South America, and especially in Central America, people lived as farmers, and built towns and cities.

American Civilizations

The most spectacular builders of North America were the Anasazi people, who lived in the southwest region of what is now the United States. They lived in cliffside 'apartment blocks' called *pueblos*. Their descendants took the name of Pueblo. The Anasazi and their neighbours, the Hohokam, grew corn, wove cotton cloth and made clay pottery.

Teotihuacan (Mexico) begins its rise to power.	AD 350
The city of Tiahuanaco (Bolivia) and Huari empire (Peru) are flourishing.	AD 600
In what is now southwest USA, the Anasazi build multi-storey houses.	AD 700
The Mayan civilization is at its most powerful for the next 200 years.	AD 700
The city of Teotihuacan is destroyed. Tiahuanaco also declines about this time.	AD 750
Rise of the Toltecs in Mexico. They build a city called Tula.	AD 900
Chichén Itzá is the most important Mayan city and religious centre.	AD 900
The Mississippian people develop a farming culture in North America.	AD 1000

Teotihuacan

In Mexico, there stood one of the biggest cities in world. It was called Teotihuacan, or 'City of the Gods', and it grew in the Teotihuacan valley from AD 350 to 750. The city had wide avenues, squares, palaces and temples. These temples were built as step pyramids, and towered more than 60 metres high. The two largest are the Pyramid of the Sun and the Pyramid of the Moon. We know little about the city and what happened in it. It was conquered by the Toltecs who built their own temple-city at Tula.

Great mountain city

Over 3,500 metres high in the Andes Mountains, not far from Lake Titicaca, was the city of Tiahuanaco. It thrived between AD 500 and 1000. The kingdom of which it was part was ruled by priest-kings, who grew rich from farming and trade with nearby states such as Huari in Peru.

△ The Maya played a ball game in which players tried to knock a rubber ball through a stone ring. The game was both a sport and a religious rite, with the ball possibly representing the Sun.

△ *A temple in the Mayan city of Chichén Itzá. The city's natural well, called a cenote, was used for sacrifices. Many Mayan treasures have been recovered from the well, which was surrounded by pyramids, temples and other buildings, including a ball court.*

Priests and gods

A Mayan priest wears an elaborate feathered headdress. The Maya worshipped many gods. Priests led ceremonies in the pyramid-temples. Sacrificial offerings were made to please the gods, who included the jaguar.

The Maya

The Maya were at their most powerful from AD 200 to 900. Their calendars date back to before 3000 BC, and they remained powerful until conquered by the Spanish in the AD 1500s.

The Maya lived in city-states, ruled by kings who ruled over a society of priests, nobles, warriors, skilled craftworkers and peasant farmers. Each city had its own sign, or emblem. Hunters in the forests brought birds' feathers, which were made into headdresses, and also jaguar skins, which were highly prized.

Mayan farmers grew beans, corn and squash. They kept turkeys for meat and bees for honey, but they had no domestic animals that were big enough to pull wheeled carts.

Cities and sacrifices

The Maya built large cities. The biggest was Tikal (Guatemala), where about 60,000 people lived. Religious ceremonies and sacrifices (involving animals and sometimes humans) were at the centre of Mayan life. Priests skilled in maths and astronomy studied the stars, the Sun and the Moon. The Maya used sign writing, and wrote on thin pieces of bark.

△ *Chac, the Maya rain god. Carved stone figures called Chac Mools have been found in Maya temples. They were probably used to make sacrificial offerings.*

" Give us a steady light, a level place
a good light, a good place,
a good life and beginning.

from THE POPUL VUH, ANONYMOUS MAYAN POEM

In the first centuries after Christ, Christianity spread from Palestine into North Africa, Asia Minor and across Europe. Further east, many people in the Arabian peninsula were still pagans, worshipping ancient gods. In this region, during the 600s, there arose a new religion – Islam.

The Rise of Islam

Islam had its roots in the Hebrew-Christian belief in one God, and its prophet was Muhammad (AD 570–632).

Muhammad's life and vision

Muhammad was born in Mecca (now in Saudi Arabia), an important trading town. After his parents died, he was raised by an uncle and became a merchant and caravan manager

Muhammad was angered by the evils he saw around him in Mecca: injustice, selfishness and the worship of pagan idols. Many religious

Probable date of Muhammad's birth.	AD 570
Muhammad begins preaching in Mecca.	AD 610
Flight to Medina, the Hegira.	AD 622
Muslims defeat the Meccans at Badr.	AD 624
Muhammad's teachings are written down in the Koran, the holy book of Islam.	AD 625
Meccans besiege Medina.	AD 627
Muhammad leads an army into Mecca and smashes the pagan idols there.	AD 630
Muhammad dies. Abu Bakr becomes the first caliph. Islam spreads beyond Arabia.	AD 632
Ummayad dynasty rules the Islamic world from Damascus.	AD 661

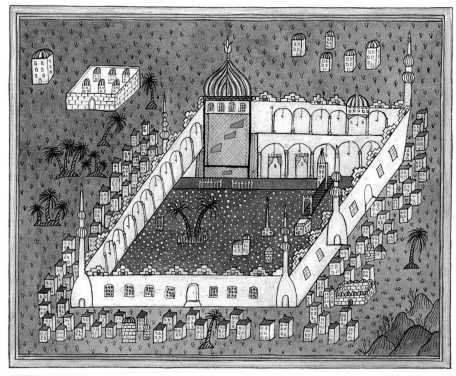

△ The old mosque at Mecca. Muhammad used to pray in the courtyard of his home. As a result, Islamic mosques have an open space where people gather five times a day to pray.

▷ The Muslims built mosques and minarets wherever the new religion took hold. One of the oldest Islamic monuments is the Dome of the Rock in Jerusalem (right), which was completed in AD 691. According to Muslim belief, Muhammad ascended to heaven from here to speak with God.

△ The people of Arabia traded by camel caravans, which broke their journeys at oases. Muhammad knew this life well. As a young man he worked as a manager for the caravans. He married his employer, a widow named Khadija.

ideas were talked over by travellers of many beliefs (including Jews and Christians) who met in the town to do business. Old beliefs were being questioned.

Muslims believe that the angel Gabriel came to Muhammad in a vision. The angel told Muhammad he must bring people to belief in the one true God, Allah, and to submission (Islam).

The birth of Islam

Muhammad began preaching, and soon got into into trouble with the authorities in Mecca. In AD 622 he left the city, hid from his enemies in a cave and then travelled across the desert to the town of Medina. This journey, known as the Hegira, begins the Muslim calendar. The Medinans welcomed him and adopted the new faith.

Many people in Mecca were determined to crush Islam. But in AD 630 Muhammad's forces entered the city in triumph. He broke up the pagan idols in the Kaaba, or shrine, but spared the Black Stone, which is still there. The Meccans submitted and Muhammad continued to preach, and live frugally, until he died in AD 632.

Mecca became the holiest city of Islam. Muhammad's teachings were written down in the Koran, the holy book of Islam.

Astronomy

Astronomy was a respected science in the Islamic world, and Baghdad and other cities had flourishing scientific communities. Arab astronomers added their own observations to those of the Babylonians and Greeks, and named many of the brightest stars.

△ Beautifully decorated tiles adorn the walls, domes and minarets of mosques throughout the Islamic world. The brightly coloured tiles feature geometric and arabesque patterns.

From the AD 500s, Japan was influenced more and more by Chinese ideas. The teachings of Confucius and Buddhism were brought to Japan. Prince Shotoku, who ruled from AD 593 to 622, strongly encouraged Chinese ways.

Fujiwara Japan

Shotoku believed that the Japanese emperor should be all-powerful, like the ruler of China. He made Buddhism the national religion, but the old Shinto religion continued to be strong, preserving a distinct Japanese identity.

Prince Shotoku's changes

Shotoku reorganized the Japanese court into 12 ranks, and set out rules which governed the behaviour of everyone from ruler to lowliest peasant. Shotoku's successors divided Japan into provinces, governed by local officials who reported directly to the emperor. In AD 794 emperor Kammu made Kyoto (then called Heian) his capital.

The Fujiwaras

In AD 858, however, the emperor lost control to a strong noble family called the Fujiwaras. The Fujiwaras had built up their power in the countryside, where they owned huge estates. Other nobles too had built up small 'empires' of their own.

The Fujiwaras gradually won control of the emperors, and of government, by marrying their daughters into the imperial family. The emperor had little real power. His Fujiwara 'adviser' gave the orders.

Reign of Prince Shotoku, called the founder of Japanese civilization.	AD 593
Shotoku sends first Japanese embassy to China.	AD 608
Earliest written works in Japanese.	AD 700
Emperor Kammu makes Kyoto his capital.	AD 794
Bronze sculptures of Buddha made at the temple of Horyuji.	AD 800s
Fujiwara family gains control over the emperor.	AD 858
The Tale of Genji was probably written about this date.	AD 1008
Feuds weaken Fujiwara control. Power shifts to the daimyos.	AD 1000s

△ At the court of the Fujiwaras, richly dressed men and women spent much of their time strolling in ornate gardens with flowering trees, artificial hills and ponds.

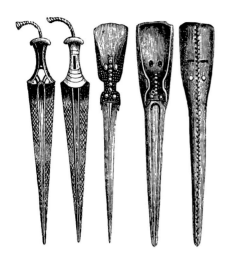

△ *Japanese daggers. Iron weapons were made in Japan from the AD 300s, and were buried in nobles' tombs, with armour and models of servants and animals.*

Samurai warriors

Japanese soldiers used iron swords and wore heavy armour. The bands of soldiers who served the land-owning lords became known as the samurai, the 'knights' of medieval Japan.

The Fujiwaras held onto power in Japan for 300 years. During this time the great estates grew bigger and stronger, until the lords ruling them were almost like kings. By the AD 1000s, these lords, who were called daimyos, led private armies of heavily armoured soldiers. These soldiers were called samurai.

Elegant court life

Fujiwara rule was based on life at court. Here, elegant courtiers wandered through beautiful gardens, or listened to poetry and stories. One of the most famous books in Japanese is *The Tale of Genji*, a long novel written by a court lady-in-waiting called Murasaki Shikibu in the early AD 1000s. Japanese writing was done with great care and skill, using a brush. The Japanese adopted Chinese writing to create their own written language, using characters to represent sounds. Only a few educated people could read Japanese.

Few ordinary people knew anything about this elegant life, unless they worked as servants at court. Most Japanese lived in small villages, as peasant farmers. They grew rice and vegetables, and caught fish from the sea. Small trading craft sailed between Japan and China, but otherwise Japan had little contact with the outside world.

△ *A wooden gate, or torii, is the symbol of Shinto, and stands outside Shinto temples. Shinto (meaning 'the way of the gods') was the traditional religion of Japan.*

Lady Koshosho, all noble and charming, she is like a weeping willow at budding time. Her style is very elegant and we all envy her manners.
DIARY OF MURASAKI SHIKIBU (c. AD 975–1031)

After the end of Han rule in AD 220, China was weak and divided until AD 581 when Yang Chien founded the Sui dynasty (a series of rulers from the same family). He ruled from the city of Chang'an and governed well encouraging agriculture and foreign trade.

Chinese Dynasties

Chinese cities were a wonder to foreign visitors. Chang'an had more than one million citizens, yet its cleanliness was startling. There were public baths, and hot water was sold in the streets for washing. Toilet facilities in houses were fairly basic, emptying into cesspits, but waste was collected in carts every evening and taken away. The Chinese habit of using toilet paper came as another surprise to visitors.

The Tang and Sung dynasties

The second Sui emperor, Yang Di, was less prudent than Yang Chien. He taxed people heavily to pay for expensive projects, such as rebuilding the Grand Canal and constructing new imperial palaces and gardens. Discontent flared into revolt. The emperor was killed and a government official named Li Yuan seized power. He founded the Tang dynasty, which lasted for almost 300 years until it was overthrown by the warlord Chu Wen in AD 907.

End of Han dynasty is followed by a period of weak rule known as Six Dynasties.	AD 220
Start of Sui dynasty.	AD 581
The printing press may have been invented in China as early as this.	AD 600
Start of Tang dynasty. Period of prosperity and progress in arts and sciences.	AD 618
Northern rebellion is led by a soldier named An Lushan.	AD 755
More rebellions, leading to the fall of the Tang dynasty in 907.	AD 875–907
The Five Dynasties and Ten Kingdoms – leaders struggle for power in China.	AD 907–960
Sung dynasty founded. China's population tops 100 million.	AD 960

△ The wheelbarrow was a Chinese invention and was used by farmers, market traders and construction workers. This typical barrow has a central wheel, unlike today's garden barrows.

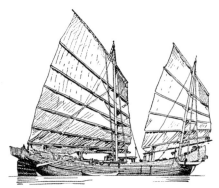

△ *A two-masted Chinese junk. Chinese ships had watertight compartments and stern rudders. With easily handled sails, they were less sinkable and more easily steered than Western vessels.*

△ *The oldest printed book known is the Diamond Sutta, a Buddhist scroll made from sheets of paper printed with woodblocks. It was made in China in AD 868.*

△ *By AD 1100 the Chinese were using magnetic compasses such as this one, with an iron needle and marked points.*

Making paper

A paper-maker at work, spreading wet pulp over a mesh frame. The invention of paper was announced by the director of the Chinese imperial workshops in AD 105. The Chinese began to use paper money under Sung rule.

For a time China was then split into five dynasties and smaller kingdoms, but in AD 960, the Sung dynasty reunited China and made their capital at Kaifeng. The Sung ruled until AD 1279. They were not as strong as the Tang emperors, but they were more technologically advanced.

Chinese culture

The Tang and Sung periods were good times for China. Painters and poets flourished, China was united and prosperous. Painters created beautiful calm landscapes, to show the harmony between people and nature. Poets such as Wang Wei, Li Po and Tu Fu wrote about love and war. Potters made delicate pottery, known as porcelain. The Chinese were the first people to print books, using wood blocks.

Trade in China moved by road and along the impressive canals. The Grand Canal connected the main rivers. Most canals were dug in level ground, so avoiding the need for locks, but in the AD 900s Chinese engineers developed the pound-lock, with gates at either end, which could be emptied or flooded to let boats pass through.

New technology

The Chinese were fascinated by machines. They invented the wheelbarrow for carrying loads, and even fitted barrows with sails to make pushing easier. They used waterwheels to mill rice and drive hammers to beat metal into shape. They knew about the magnetic compass, and their ships had stern rudders (still unknown in the West). Chinese soldiers had the best crossbows in the world, and also a range of smoke and fire weapons. Most alarming of all to an enemy were rockets, which began to be used in the 900s, and 'fireguns' – bamboo tubes filled with gunpowder.

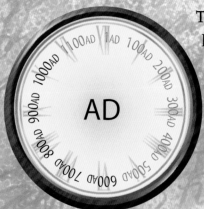

AD

The advance of Islam seemed unstoppable in the late 600s. The Byzantine and Persian empires could not halt the armies of Islam, and nor could Egypt. By AD 700 Muslims controlled most of the North African coast, and ships patrolled the Mediterranean Sea and Indian Ocean.

Muslim Empires

Abu Bakr becomes first caliph.	AD 632
Caliph Omar is murdered and is succeeded by Otham, leader of the Ummayad.	AD 644
Othman is murdered and the Shiite leader Ali becomes caliph.	AD 656
Ali is murdered. The Islamic capital moves from Mecca to Damascus.	AD 661
Caliph Abdalmalik sets up new government system for the Islamic empire.	AD 685–705
Franks defeat Muslims at battle of Poitiers to halt their advance into Europe.	AD 732
The Abbasid dynasty is founded.	AD 750
Harun al-Rashid unites the Islamic empire.	AD 786
Turkish Seljuks seize power in Baghdad.	AD 1000s

Muslims from Morocco invaded Spain, but the advance of Islam into western Europe was stopped in AD 732 by the Frankish army of Charles Martel.

Life under Ummayad rule

Under the rule of the Ummayad family in Damascus there were four classes of citizens: Arabian Muslims; new converts; Christians, Jews and Mandaeans (a Persian sect); and slaves. The new converts included people from Egypt, Syria, Persia and Asia Minor. They adopted Arab ways, but brought to the Arabs a wealth of new learning in philosopy, medicine, art and science.

Islam had been born in the desert. The Ummayad court was a more sophisticated world where music and gambling were tolerated. One caliph married a Christian. Another spent most of his time horse racing.

The Abbasid Empire

Ummayad rule got weaker, but lasted until the mid-700s. Then Abu al Abbas, a descendant of Muhammad, founded a new dynasty – the Abbasids. His followers raised an army in Persia, and rallied the supporters of the dead caliph Ali to their cause. After a terrible battle lasting nine

▷ A scene from The Thousand and One Nights, a collection of stories set in the Baghdad court of Harun al-Rashid, the most famous of the Abbasid rulers. In these stories, collected from around the eastern world, characters such as Sinbad and Aladdin appear.

△ *An Arab astronomer's drawing of the star group, or constellation, of Orion (the Hunter). Like the Greeks, Arab scientists drew constellations as human figures, animals or objects.*

▷ *Arab trading ships sailed across the Indian Ocean to India and Indonesia, and farther eastwards as far as China.*

days, they captured Damascus. Most of the Ummayad ruling family was murdered, and the new rulers soon moved their capital to Baghdad (in what is now Iraq).

Arabic was the common language throughout most of the Islamic world. By AD 786 the court of the caliph Harun al-Rashid at Baghdad was one of the most splendid in the world. Trading ships sailed to and from China, and the warehouses along the River Tigris were stocked with rare and wonderful goods from Africa, India and the Far East. Medicine and science were in advance of anything known in Europe. There were slaves from Africa, and even Scandinavia.

Rival rulers, however, claimed independence in various parts of this empire. Baghdad itself came under threat in the 11th century, from invaders.

The Seljuk Empire

The Seljuks were descendants of nomadic Turks from central Asia. They took their name from a chief named Seljuk. They charged into the western Islamic world in the early AD 1000s. Their leader Toghril Beg captured Baghdad. His nephew Alp Arslan attacked the city of Constantinople and defeated the Byzantine army in AD 1071.

The Seljuks

The Turkish Seljuks were superb horsemen, riding with stirrups and firing bows at the gallop. Known as 'the men of the sword', they added new strength to Islam, which was governed by 'the men of the law'.

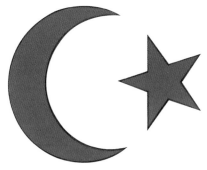

△ *The crescent moon and star became important symbols in Islam, and were often incorporated into architecture and other designs. The Islamic year calendar is based on the cycle of the Moon.*

AD

After the fall of the Roman Empire, the Christian church provided the only stable government in Europe. It was weakened by its division, between the west (Rome) and the east (Constantinople), and faced growing pressure from the spread of Islam.

Monastic Life

The Christian faith spread slowly among the pagan peoples of western and northern Europe, who were called 'heathens' by Christians. Its teachings were spread by missionaries, such as Patrick, Augustine and Boniface. Missionaries travelled to the British Isles, Germany, Scandinavia and Russia, converting the local rulers and building churches. It was a slow business, and parts of northern Europe were not Christian until the beginning of the second millennium.

Egyptian missionaries preach in Ethiopia.	AD 350
St Patrick preaches Christianity in Ireland.	AD 450
St Columba founds a monastery on the island of Iona.	AD 500s
St Benedict of Nursia sets out the rules for Western monks.	AD 480–543
Monte Cassino in Italy is the first abbey in Europe.	AD 529
Pope Gregory sends Augustine to convert the English.	AD 596
Augustine founds the first English Benedictine monastery at Canterbury.	AD 596
Boniface preaches to the Saxons in Germany.	c. AD 700
Edward the Confessor starts to build Westminster Abbey.	AD 1042

Christian communities took on the work of teaching the faith, education and healing, at a time when governments themselves had very little power. In this work, monasteries came to play an important part.

Saint Benedict's rules

In the early Christian world, very religious people had sometimes gone off to live on their own as hermits, to

▷ A monk at work on an illuminated manuscript (handwritten book). The work was slow and painstaking, but worthwhile because it was another way to show dedication to God.

△ The monastery at Mont Saint-Michel in France was built by Benedictine monks in AD 966. It stands on a tiny island in Normandy, linked by causeway to the French mainland.

△ Monks spent part of their time teaching young boys, who would in time become monks themselves. A monk's day was regulated by hours of work, rest and worship.

△ An 'illuminated' letter from the page of a medieval manuscript. Monastery artists and scribes decorated the pages of their books with these beautifully coloured 'illuminations'.

Celtic Christians

Elaborate carvings were made on Celtic crosses, the distinctive symbol of the Celtic Christians. They founded monasteries in the north of Britain. One of the first, at Lindisfarne, was founded in AD 635 by a monk named Aidan.

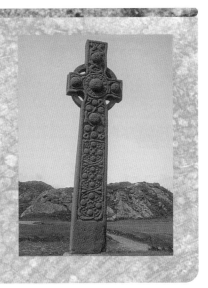

meditate and pray. Others formed strict communities, where they lived apart, praying and studying the Bible, hoping to avoid the 'sins' of town life. These communities became monasteries.

In the AD 500s, an Italian named Benedict of Nursia drew up a set of rules for monks (people in monasteries). All monks must be poor, unmarried and obedient. Monks wore simple robes, shaved their heads, and shared all their the daily tasks.

Monasteries were for men only. Religious women joined orders of their own, and became nuns. Each monastery was led by an abbot, and the largest ones became centres not only of religious life but also of local power. Some abbots had as much power as any nobleman, controlling farms, trades and even private armies.

The daily round

Monks went to eight church services every day. They ate their meals in the refectory, the dining room, often in silence while one monk read from the Bible or some other religious book. They grew their food, reared farm animals, baked bread and brewed beer. They made their clothes and furniture, and built their own churches. They also looked after the sick.

There is no salvation outside the Church.
Love the sinner but hate the sin.
Love and do what you will.

ST. AUGUSTINE OF HIPPO (AD 354-430)

St. Augustine was born in what is now Tunisia in Africa. He was one of the most important men in the early Christian Church.

In the late AD 300s the Roman army was hard pressed to fight off waves of barbarian invasions. Troops in distant outposts, such as the British Isles, were needed to defend the empire, and by AD 410 the last Roman soldiers had left England for mainland Europe.

Britain after the Romans

The Romans had hired warriors from northwest Europe (Germany and Denmark) to help defend the coasts of England against pirates and raiding bands (many of whom were Germans themselves). Without the Roman army to protect them, the Roman Britons of England were unable to prevent these mercenaries, and any new bands of invaders, from taking over land they wanted.

Roman army has left Roman Britain by this date.	AD 410
Possible date of 'King Arthur', leader of the Britons.	AD 500
Augustine arrives to convert the English to Christianity.	AD 597
Death of Redwald, king of East Anglia. Sutton Hoo ship burial.	c. AD 627
Lifetime of English monk Bede, who wrote a history of the English people.	AD 673–735
Offa of Mercia is overlord of all England.	AD 780
First Viking attacks on England.	AD 787
Kenneth MacAlpin is first king of a united Scotland.	AD 843
Rhodri Mawr is Prince of Wales.	AD 844

The newcomers were a mixture of peoples – Angles, Saxons, Jutes, Frisians – who became known as the 'English'. There were also raiders from the north, Picts and Scots, who attacked northern England.

The Saxon settlement

The invaders came to England to find land to farm. They were well armed and tough, and drove away many Britons, who moved into western England and Wales, taking their Christianity with them. The pagan newcomers took over their farms but also set about clearing new land. They felled trees, ploughed the land and built wooden houses.

The new English were suspicious of Roman-British civilization and avoided the towns. Gradually these towns fell into decay. Roads were no longer used and Roman villas, their owners gone, became ruins – empty reminders of a vanished way of life.

△ *A Scots warrior. The Scots' leader, Kenneth MacAlpin, was the first king to rule the land we now call Scotland.*

Sutton Hoo

Artefacts from the Sutton Hoo burial site include a gold belt, a sword and shield. There are also several items of jewellery. Finally, there was a sceptre and standard which must have belonged to the dead King Redwald.

The English kings

By AD 600, the English had set up several small kingdoms. These included Kent, East Anglia, Essex, Sussex and Wessex ('the lands of the East, South and West Saxons'), Mercia and Northumbria.

The most powerful ruler among the English kings was acknowledged as 'bretwalda', or supreme king. The Sutton Hoo ship burial, discovered in AD 1939, is almost certainly the monument to King Redwald of East Anglia, who was bretwalda in the AD 620s, and who died in AD 627. The strongest English king of the AD 700s was Offa of Mercia.

Western and northern Britain

In Wales there were four British kingdoms: Gywnedd, Dyfed, Powys and Gwent. These were independent under their own princes. In the west of England was the kingdom of Dumnonia. In the far north, the Picts ruled Pictavia and fought the Scots who ruled in the west. By the AD 800s, the Scots, under Kenneth MacAlpin, claimed to rule the Picts as well.

△ *Saxon farmers harvested grain with sickles and pitchforks. The Saxons tilled old Roman fields and ploughed new land, but abandoned the Roman villas.*

At this period … Britain, being deprived … of all her warlike stores, and of the flower of her army, was exposed to the ravages of her enemies on every side.

ECCLESIASTICAL HISTORY, ST BEDE (AD 731)

Bede was a monk in the AD 700s. He wrote an important book called the Ecclesiastical History of the English People.

△ *The iron helmet found in the ship burial at Sutton Hoo is one of many treasures unearthed by archaeologists at the site in Suffolk.*

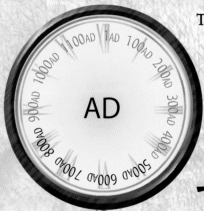

AD

The Franks emerged from the ruins of the Roman Empire in AD 476 as the dominant people of western Europe. Their leader Clovis enlarged his lands around the River Rhine (Germany) by wars. By AD 540 the Franks ruled most of the old Roman province of Gaul (France, named after the Franks).

The Franks

The first Frankish ruling family is known as the Merovingian dynasty, after Clovis's grandfather Meroveus. Clovis became a Christian. He made Paris his capital city. Most of the Franks were peasant farmers, who lived on lands ruled by nobles. The peasants raised food, doing the seasonal tasks of ploughing, sowing and harvesting. They also had to fight for their lord when he went to war. Frankish lords fought to win new land and shared the spoils of conquest with their soldiers. This Frankish system of land-holding and service was the beginning of the feudal system in Europe.

Clovis becomes king of the Franks.	AD 481
Franks defeat the last great Roman army in the West at the battle of Soissons.	AD 486
Franks control most of Gaul and Germany.	AD 540
Pepin the Short founds the Carolingian dynasty.	AD 751
Charlemagne born.	c. AD 742
Charlemagne rules the Franks.	AD 771
Charlemagne fights Muslims in Spain. The Frankish army is attacked at Roncesvalles.	AD 778
Charlemagne is crowned emperor of the West by Pope Leo III.	AD 800
Charlemagne dies.	AD 814

The Carolingians

The Merovingian kings actually had less power than their 'mayors of the royal palace', officials who traditionally came from two families. The winner of a power struggle between these families was Pepin of Herstal, who ruled the

▷ Charlemagne was very tall and a man of enormous energy. He could not write, but he did learn to read Latin. He liked to listen as books were read to him.

▷ Frankish soldiers head for battle. Under Charlemagne, the Frankish Empire expanded greatly, taking in neighbouring Bavaria and Lombardy. The Franks finally conquered Saxony after around 30 years of bitter fighting.

△ The sword of Charlemagne. The favourite weapons of Frankish soldiers were the lance and the sword.

Franks even though he was not their king. Pepin's son was Charles Martel, whose army defeated the Muslim invaders of southern Europe in AD 632. Charles Martel's son was another Pepin, Pepin the Short, and he made himself king.

Pepin the Short's son Charles became the most famous of all Frankish rulers. He was called Carolus Magnus (Charles the Great), or Charlemagne in old French. The 'Carolingian' dynasty is named after him.

Charlemagne's empire

When Pepin died, his sons Carloman and Charlemagne shared power until Carloman died. Then Charlemagne set out and won new wars of conquest in the Netherlands, Germany and Italy. When he defeated pagans, such as the Saxons of Germany, he forced them to become Christians like himself.

Charlemagne wanted to govern well. His capital of Aachen, called 'a second Rome', was rich and dazzling, yet he chose to live simply. No other ruler in Europe was so famous or magnificent, and on Christmas Day in 800 the pope crowned Charlemagne Holy Roman Emperor.

New writing

This is a sample of Carolingian script, the clear and more easily written style of writing that was introduced during the reign of Charlemagne. The actual text is written in Latin.

△ The horn of Roland, a Frankish hero killed at the battle of Roncesvalles in AD 778.

AD

The power of the English kingdoms ebbed and flowed as first one, then another, became dominant. By AD 800 the strongest English kingdom was Wessex. But it faced a threat from yet more invaders who saw in England a good place to settle – the Vikings.

Alfred the Great

The Vikings came from Norway, Sweden and Denmark. The first Viking ships appeared off the southern English coast in AD 787, according to the history known as the Anglo-Saxon Chronicle, which was begun in the reign of Alfred.

Northern Britain too felt the fury of these marauding Norsemen, or Danes as the English called them. Vikings raided and looted the rich monasteries of Northumbria. Ships loaded with families and farm animals also crossed the North Sea, and Viking farmers and traders settled in Orkney, in Ireland and the Isle of Man.

A fight for survival

In AD 850 a huge fleet of 350 Viking ships appeared in the River Thames. That winter a Viking army camped in southeast England for the first time. Such mass attacks posed a threat to the survival of the English kingdoms.

East Anglia, Northumbria and Mercia were all ravaged by Viking armies in the AD 860s. The Christian king of East Anglia, King Edmund, was murdered for refusing to give up his faith. In AD 871 Wessex was attacked. Its new king was the young and untested Alfred, the fifth of four brothers, each of whom had been king before him.

Alfred's wars and peace

Alfred's first campaigns were failures, and he had to retreat and hide in the

First Vikings land in England.	AD 787
Alfred is born.	AD 849
A great army of Vikings attacks England.	AD 865
Vikings kill King Edmund of East Anglia.	AD 869
Alfred becomes king of Wessex.	AD 871
Alfred captures London and fortifies the city.	AD 886
Alfred dies. His son Edward becomes king (to AD 924).	AD 899
Athelstan, Alfred's grandson, rules English and Vikings in England.	AD 924
Reign of Edgar, the high point of Anglo-Saxon rule in England.	AD 959–975

△ Alfred had fought at sea himself, and ordered the building of ships for the first English navy. The new ships were similar to the Viking longships, but bigger and faster.

The Danelaw

The lands in eastern England settled by the Vikings became known as the Danelaw. The English at the time referred to the invaders as 'Danes'. In places, Viking settlers mingled with the local people.

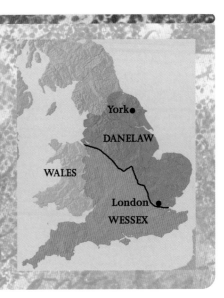

York

DANELAW

WALES

London

WESSEX

△ *Alfred is said to have made candle clocks to time his working day, which was divided between government, prayer and learning.*

marshes of Somerset. Rallying his forces, he defeated the Vikings at the battle of Edington and made a treaty with them. The Viking leader Guthrum agreed to become a Christian. In return, Alfred allowed the Vikings to settle in East Anglia.

Alfred was now recognized as king of all the English. He set about making his kingdom strong enough to resist future Viking attacks. He built a navy. He built forts and fortified towns called burhs to protect the countryside. He rebuilt the defences of London. He organized a system of 'call-up' in time of war – a farmer had to supply two soldiers for every plough on his land. The army was divided into two groups: one armed and ready to fight, the other working on farms and guarding the forts.

Law-maker and scholar

Alfred issued new laws, to end the feuds which caused bloodshed between families and to give more protection to the weak against the strong. He divided his kingdom into shires governed by ealdormen.

Alfred invited foreign scholars to his court. He was determined to educate his people, and spent many hours translating books from Latin into English. For his many achievements, he is the only English king honoured with the title 'the Great'.

△ *The Alfred jewel was found near Athelney in Somerset in AD 1693. It may be part of a bookmark. On it are the words "Alfred had me made" in Latin.*

Then began I ... to turn into English the book that is named in Latin *Pastoralis* ... one-while word for word, another-while meaning for meaning.

ALFRED THE GREAT (AD 849–899)

Alfred was the most important law-maker among England's early kings.

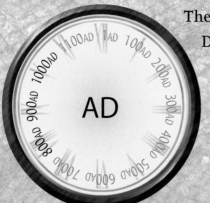

AD

The Vikings came from Scandinavia (Norway, Denmark and Sweden). Their homeland of mountains, fjords and forests offered little spare farmland for a growing population. So, many Vikings went abroad in search of new lands to settle.

The Vikings

The Vikings were farmers, but also fierce warriors, and their first impact on western Europe was a violent one. Norwegians and Danes began to sail across the North Sea in the late AD 700s, raiding the coasts of Britain and mainland Europe. They raided churches and towns, carrying off loot and slaves. Their raids caused panic, and rulers tried to buy off the invaders with gold. This only encouraged the Vikings to come back for more.

The trading town of Hedeby in Denmark is founded.	AD 790s
First reported Viking raid on England.	AD 787
Vikings begin to settle in the Baltic region and Russia.	AD 860
Vikings reach Iceland.	AD 874
Vikings are given Normandy to prevent further attacks on France.	AD 911
Danish Vikings become Christians.	AD 960
Erik the Red discovers Greenland.	AD 982
Leif Eriksson lands in North America.	AD 1003
A Dane, Cnut, becomes king of England.	AD 1016

Trade and home life

Viking towns such as Kaupang in Norway and Hedeby in Denmark flourished on deals in furs, reindeer antlers and walrus ivory. These materials were exchanged for weapons, jewels and pottery.

Viking home life was based on farming and fishing. Several generations (including uncles and cousins) often shared one single-roomed house made of wood, stone or turf. A good sword was passed down from father to son.

Many of the Vikings' gods were the same pagan gods of the Germans and English. The most important was one-eyed Odin, but most people's favourite was Thor, the thunder god who brandished his hammer.

△ Ships lie beached beside a Viking town, with wooden houses thatched with straw. Vikings made long journeys by ship and overland to trade.

△ Both Viking men and women dressed in hard-wearing clothing made from linen or woollen cloth. They wore shoes made from leather.

Longships

The Viking longships were fast and strong enough to cross oceans. They had a long, slender hull with a single mast and sail.

Intrepid voyagers

Sailing west into the Atlantic Ocean, Norwegian Vikings settled in Iceland (AD 874) and Greenland (AD 982), and landed in North America in AD 1003. Swedish Vikings crossed the Baltic to the important trade towns of Kiev and Novgorod, and travelled on eastwards to the Black Sea. Greek and Arab merchants called the northerners 'Rus' – which is how Russia got its name.

Vikings could be found in Sicily, Baghdad and Constantinople. Trade goods from such faraway places have been found in Jorvik (York) in England and in Dublin in Ireland.

Leaders and government

The leader of each community was the richest landowner, or jarl. He shared his wealth, entertaining his warriors and servants to feasts and songs in his great hall. The most powerful leaders called themselves kings. They tried to settle blood feuds between enemies, which were very common.

Viking free men met in assemblies called 'things' to settle disputes about crimes or land disagreements. Laws passed down from generation to generation. A person who refused to obey the rules of the 'thing' was an outlaw, and anyone might kill him.

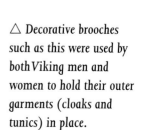

△ Decorative brooches such as this were used by both Viking men and women to hold their outer garments (cloaks and tunics) in place.

> Since tonight the wind is high/ The sea's white mane a fury/ I need not fear the hordes of Hell/ Coursing the Irish Channel.

ON THE VIKING RAIDS, ANONYMOUS

AD

By the AD 1000s trade routes between Europe and Asia were well established. Much of this trade went by sea. People traded in slaves and furs, gold and silver, ivory and precious stones, silk and carpets, glass and leatherwork.

Trade and Towns

Arab dhows sailed to India and East Africa, Chinese junks to the islands of Indonesia and Japan. Viking ships crossed the Atlantic to Iceland, Greenland and North America. The Vikings founded small settlements. In Iceland, settlers met in the Althing – Europe's oldest democratic assembly.

Paper-making spreads from China into the Islamic world.	AD 750
Porcelain is first made in China.	AD 900
Trade treaties are made between Kiev and Constantinople.	AD 907
An Arab scholar Al-Masudi travels the East African coast as far south as Mozambique.	AD 916
Rise of the kingdom of Ghana in Africa and its chief city Kumbi Saleh.	AD 920
Woodblock printing of cheap books in China.	AD 950
First Viking sighting of North American mainland.	AD 1000
Ghana kingdom controls trade routes across the Sahara in Africa.	AD 1000
Leif Eriksson lands in North America.	AD 1003

By land and sea

Many sea craft were small, with oars, and could navigate rivers, so river towns were often busy ports, London and Viking Jorvik (York), for example. There was regular trade between Vikings in Jorvik and Dublin in Ireland, with Viking towns in Scandinavia.

Few poor people ever left their home village except perhaps to go to market. But scholars, soldiers, merchants and kings travelled far, even though roads were poor. Charlemagne travelled widely around his empire. King Alfred went from England to Rome as a boy. Most journeys were made on foot, or on horseback, and were slow. Travellers followed well-used

△ Merchants exchange goods in a busy street in Viking Jorvik (modern York) in England. These men are trading in furs, which were one of the main exports of Jorvik at this time.

▷ Caravans carrying gold, salt and slaves followed the long trails across the Sahara Desert. There was trade between the cities of West Africa and those of North Africa, Egypt and Arabia. The routes taken by Muslim pilgrims to Mecca in Arabia were also important.

trade routes, where some safety from bandits might be expected. The most famous was the Silk Road, the long trade route overland from China to the west.

How peoples saw themselves

By AD 1000 the Christian peoples of Europe were taught to see themselves as belonging to 'Christendom' – the Christian world. In its empire, Islam had unified peoples who shared not only a religion but also language, science and art.

To an Easterner, Western civilization appeared much less sophisticated. An Arab ambassador seeing Vikings in Russia thought them impressive ("as tall as date palms"), but uncivilized – they ate like animals, lived in crude houses, and worshipped idols.

Civilizations apart

With their canals, fine houses, markets and restaurants, Chinese cities were unrivalled. Yet, China remained aloof, caring little for what went on in the barbarian world beyond its frontiers. The peoples of North and South America too remained outside the growing cultural exchange.

△ Odin, the god of battle and death, was one of the principal gods worshipped by the Vikings. He was the ruler of Asgard, the heavenly home of the gods.

Silk traders

For many years the Chinese were the only people that knew how to make silk. European traders would make the long journey to China to take silk back to Europe, where it was an expensive luxury.

△ A pottery figure of an Armenian merchant, made in China during the Tang dynasty (AD 618–907).

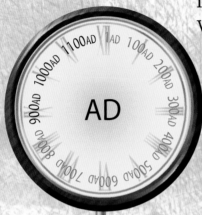

In the AD 900s England was again attacked by Vikings. King Ethelred (AD 978–1016) tried to buy off the invaders with bribes. His people had to pay higher taxes to raise the money. But the idea of bribes did not work either.

Norman Conquest

In AD 1013 the Danish king Sweyn Forkbeard made himself king of England, and the unpopular Ethelred fled to Normandy in France. In AD 1016 Sweyn's son Cnut became king. During his reign, which lasted until AD 1035, England was ruled as part of Cnut's empire, which included Denmark and Norway. Cnut was a good king, but his two sons had brief reigns, and England's next ruler brought confusion.

Edward the Confessor

The new king was Edward, known as the Confessor, son of the exiled Etheltred. He was more Norman than English, and very religious – he built the first Westminster Abbey.

Power was in the hands of the English earls, like the scheming Godwine of Wessex. Edward married Godwine's daughter, but they had no children. So when Edward died in AD 1066, there was no obvious heir. The witan, or council, of England chose Earl Godwine's son, Harold, as king.

Rivals for a crown

There were two other claimants. One was Harold Hardrada, king of Norway. The other was William, Duke of Normandy, a distant relative of Edward the Confessor. William claimed that Harold had sworn to

Viking leader Rollo is given Normandy. Normandy is later ruled by dukes.	AD 911
King Cnut, ruler of England, Norway and Denmark, dies.	AD 1035
Death of Harthacnut, last Danish king of England.	AD 1042
King Macbeth of Scotland is killed by Malcom Canmore, who later becomes king.	AD 1057
Harold, son of Godwine, and his brother Tostig fight the Welsh.	AD 1063
Harold is shipwrecked in Normandy.	AD 1064
Edward the Confessor sees the completion of Westminster Abbey.	AD 1065
Harold is king. Normans win battle of Hastings. William becomes king.	AD 1066

△ The Normans built castles to defend their newly won lands and subdue the conquered English. Each castle stood on an earth mound, or motte. A wooden tower was built on top. At the foot of the mound was a stockade, or bailey, inside which were stables, houses for soldiers, stores and a kitchen.

△ *William of Normandy ruled England from AD 1066 to 1087. He claimed that Edward the Confessor promised him the throne in AD 1051. He also said that Harold (who was shipwrecked in France in AD 1064) had sworn to accept this.*

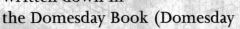

Domesday Book

In AD 1085 William I ordered a survey of land in England. The findings were written down in the Domesday Book (Domesday means 'Day of Judgement'). It is the best record we have of life in England between AD 1066 and 1088, naming about 13,000 towns and villages.

back his claim. This may or may not be true. Hardrada and William were both tough soldiers, and both prepared to attack England to seize the throne.

Two battles and a conquest

The Norwegians landed first, in the north of England. Harold defeated them at the battle of Stamford Bridge near York on September 25. Both Harold Hardrada and Tostig were killed. Then news came that William's ships had landed in Sussex, and Harold at once dashed south to fight them.

The crucial battle was fought only 19 days later, on October 14 at Senlac Hill, north of Hastings. The English, who fought on foot, resisted bravely as the Norman cavalry charged their wall of shields, and archers fired showers of arrows at them. In the end, Harold was killed, the shield wall broke, and the Normans won.

The Normans rule

William declared himself king. He was crowned in Westminster Abbey on Christmas Day. The English nobles lost their lands. French became the language of government. William and his barons built castles to guard their new land. A new age was beginning.

▷ *The story of William's invasion and the battle of Hastings is told in 72 scenes in the Bayeux Tapestry. The embroidery is about 50 cm wide and 70 m long. It was made on the orders of William's half-brother.*

Timeline and Reference Section

	before 10,000 BC	10,000 to 5000 BC	5000 to 3000 BC
Events and Rulers	c. 30,000 BC Neanderthals die out. First modern humans settle North America, from Asia. 16,000 BC Last Ice Age ends.	Land bridge joining Britain and France is covered by sea. First farmers set up settled communities, with leaders who become the first kings.	Sahara region, once fertile, starts to dry up. First important settlements around the Tigris and Euphrates rivers. 4236 BC First date in the Egyptian calendar. c. 3500 BC First Chinese walled towns.
Exploration	40,000 BC Cro-Magnons move into Europe. 35,000 BC People reach America and Australia.	10,000 BC People reach tip of S.America. 6000 BC Catal Huyuk traders travel overland.	4000 BC People reach Pacific Islands by boat.
Art and Science	25,000 BC Cave people make clay figures. Cave paintings in France and Spain.	Sahara rock paintings. Pottery decorated with geometric designs. Metalwork in Near East.	c. 3600 BC Earliest known map, in Sumer. *Epic of Gilgamesh*, famous Sumerian poem.
Technology	c.2,000,000 BC Early people use pebble tools. 500,000 BC People first learn how to make fire.	8000 BC Coracles and dugout canoes used. First clay pots. Metal tools made of copper.	c. 4000 BC Tin and copper mixed to make bronze in Near East. Invention of the wheel.
Religion and Ideas	Prehistoric people bury their dead with some kind of religious ceremony.	Sheep used in religious sacrifices in Near East. Pictures and models of bulls at Catal Huyuk.	Sumerians tell stories of a great flood. 3760 BC First date in the Jewish calendar.
Daily Life	15,000 BC People live in caves, tents or stick shelters. They make clothes of animal skins.	10,000 BC Farming starts in the Near East. 9000 BC Wheat and barley are grown.	5000 BC Towns grow into the first city-states. 3000 BC Sumerians make bread and beer.

3000 to 2000 BC	2000 to 1000 BC	1000 to 500 BC	
3100 BC First dynastic period. Egypt is united under one king, Menes. 2750 BC Rise of Indus Valley civilization. 2686–2160 BC Old kingdom in Egypt. Pyramids built at Giza. 2360 BC Sargon of Akkad begins conquest of Sumeria.	c. 1750 BC Indus Valley civilization collapses. c. 1500 BC Rise of Shang dynasty, China. 1361–1352 BC Reign of Tutankhamun. 1450 BC Volcano destroys Minoan Crete. 1250 BC Trojan War. 1020 BC Saul is the first king of Israel.	900 BC Kingdom of Kush is independent from Egypt. 814 BC Phoenicians found Carthage. 753 BC Traditional date for founding of Rome. 689 BC Babylon destroyed by Assyrians. 539 BC Cyrus the Great conquers Babylon.	**Events and Rulers**
Traders explore Aegean in canoe-like vessels. People from central Asia move into Europe.	About 1,500 Hebrews journey from Mesopotamia to Palestine.	700 BC Phoenicians found colony at Utica. Bantu people spread to East Africa.	**Exploration**
Harps and flutes are first made.	Babylonians invent a counting system based on 60. First Chinese writing.	776 BC First recorded Olympic Games. Hanging Gardens of Babylon built.	**Art and Science**
Use of bronze in China to make weapons. 2780 BC Step pyramid built at Saqqara, Egypt.	Water clocks, sand glasses and sundials used to measure time. Hittites smelt iron.	Kites invented by the Chinese. Assyrians attack city walls with siege towers.	**Technology**
Egyptians believe in an afterlife. They make mummies of people and animals.	1500 BC Rig Vedas, early Hindu holy songs, written in India.	500s BC Confucius teaches in China. c. 563–483 BC Life of Buddha.	**Religion and Ideas**
2600 BC Egyptians use papyrus for writing. 2000 BC Jomon people, Japan, live in pit houses.	Chinese tell fortunes with oracle bones. Phoenicians trade dye made of murex shells.	Persians begin writing on parchment. c. 700 BC Coins are first used in Lydia.	**Daily Life**

	500 to 1 BC	AD 1 to 200	AD 200 to 500
Events and Rulers	510 BC Roman Republic founded. 500 BC Achaemenid Empire in Persia. 400 BC Nok culture in West Africa. 356–323 BC Alexander the Great. 214 BC Great Wall of China built. 44 BC Julius Caesar dies.	AD 14 Death of Augustus (Octavian), first Roman emperor. AD 43 Romans invade Britain. AD 61 Boudicca leads revolt against Romans. AD 70 Romans destroy Jerusalem. AD 79 Pompeii destroyed by volcano.	AD 220 End of Han rule in China, which is split into three states. AD 320 Gupta Empire in India. Golden age of Hindu culture. AD 350 Teotihuacan begins rise to power. Rise of Mayas. AD 395 Division of Roman Empire.
Exploration	AD 470 Hanno sails by the west coast of Africa. AD 100 Silk Road links Asia and the Near East.	Romans establish trade links with China. c. AD 100 Settlers reach the Hawaiian islands.	Barbarians move into western Europe. Settlers from Germany cross the North Sea.
Art and Science	477 BC Start of Athens' Golden Age. 429 BC Birth of Greek philosopher Plato.	AD 1 First history of China completed. AD 100s Romans enjoy open-air theatre.	Classical art in the West declines. Byzantine art starts to flourish.
Technology	c. 200 BC Greeks make the Archimedean screw for raising water. Crossbow used in war.	Roman engineers use cement and concrete. AD 50 Pyramid of the Sun built in Mexico.	AD 300 Stirrup for riding in use in Asia. Chinese use rudders to steer sailing ships.
Religion and Ideas	Celts bury their dead in graves with chariots. 200s BC Buddhism spreads in India.	AD 29 Probable date of crucifixion of Jesus. AD 48 Buddhism reaches China.	AD 380 Egyptians take Christianity to Axum. AD 450 St Patrick preaches in Ireland.
Daily Life	400 BC Greeks develop democracy and public schools. Celts live in hillforts.	Chinese write on paper. They use wheelbarrows. Romans eat sugar and build public baths.	Maya build cities in Central America. China has the world's biggest cities, with restaurants.

AD 500 TO 700

AD 519 Kingdom of Wessex founded.
AD 527–565 Justinian and Theodora rule Byzantine Empire.
AD 535 End of Gupta rule in northern India.
AD 540 Franks control most of Gaul and Germany.
AD 618 Tang dynasty.

Easter Island is settled by people from Polynesia, crossing the sea in canoes or rafts.

AD 500 Indians devise modern numerals. Chinese invent porcelain.

c. AD 600 Windmill invented in Persia and Turkey.
Lateen sails on ships.

AD 529 Monte Cassino is first abbey in Europe.
AD 570 Probable date of Muhammad's birth.

AD 700 The Anasazi build multi-storey houses, and grow corn. Chinese use canal boats.

AD 700 TO 900

AD 700 Rise of Ghana Empire in Africa.
AD 711 Muslims conquer Spain.
AD 750 The city of Teotihuacan is destroyed.
AD 750 Abbasid dynasty is founded.
AD 787 First Viking attacks on Britain.

Arabs trade across Indian Ocean.
AD 874 Vikings settle in Iceland.

AD 700s First printing in China.
AD late 700s Book of Kells in Britain.

Arabs learn paper-making from Chinese.
c. AD 800 Stirrups spread to the West.

AD 826 First Christian mission to Scandinavia.
AD 864 Bulgars and Serbs become Christian.

Feudal system of strip farming in Europe.
Islamic education spreads in Middle East.

AD 900 TO 1100

AD 900 Rise of the Toltecs in Mexico.
AD 911 Vikings control Normandy.
AD 960 Sung dynasty in China.
AD 1000s Seljuks seize power in Baghdad.
AD 1066 Battle of Hastings. The Normans conquer England.

AD 916 Arabs trade along E. African coast.
AD 1003 Leif Eriksson lands in North America.

AD 1008 *The Tale of Genji* is written.
First stone abbeys and cathedrals in Europe.

Magnetic compass reaches the West.
Chinese use gunpowder rockets.

AD 966 Mont St Michel monastery in France built by the Benedictines.

AD 900s Burhs (Saxon towns) in England.
after AD 1000 Normans build stone castles.

Events and Rulers

Exploration

Art and Science

Technology

Religion and Ideas

Daily Life

Kings of England

Saxons

Egbert	ad 827–839
Ethelwulf	ad 839–858
Ethelbald	ad 858–860
Ethelbert	ad 860–866
Ethelred I	ad 866–871
Alfred the Great	ad 871–899
Edward the Elder	ad 899–924
Athelstan	ad 924–939
Edmund	ad 939–946
Edred	ad 946–955
Edwy	ad 955–959
Edgar	ad 959–975
Edward the Martyr	ad 975–978
Ethelred II the Unready	
	ad 978–1016
Edmund Ironside	ad 1016

Danes

Canute	ad 1016–1035
Harold I Harefoot	ad 1035–1040
Hardicanute	ad 1040–1042

Saxons

Edward the Confessor	
	ad 1042–1066
Harold II	ad 1066

Normans

William I the Conqueror	
	ad 1066–1087
William I	ad 1087–1100

Rulers of Scotland

Malcolm II	ad 1005–1034
Duncan I	ad 1034–1040
Macbeth	ad 1040–1057
Malcolm III Canmore	
	ad 1057–1093
Donald Bane	ad 1093–1094
Duncan II	ad 1094
Donald Bane (restored)	
	ad 1094–1097
Edgar	ad 1097–1107

Notable Roman Emperors

Augustus (Octavian)	
	27 bc–ad 14
Tiberius	ad 14–37
Caligula	ad 37–41
Claudius	ad 41–54
Nero	ad 54–68
Vespasian	ad 69–79
Trajan	ad 98–117
Hadrian	ad 117–138
Marcus Aurelius	ad 161–180
Diocletian	ad 284–305
Constantine I	ad 308–337
Theodosius I the Great	
	ad 378–395

Chinese dynasties

Hsia	before 2200 bc to 1500 bc
Shang	1500–1122 bc
Zhou	1122–256 bc
Qin	221–207 bc
Han	202 bc to ad 220 (with break)
Three kingdoms and six dynasties	ad 220–581
Sui	ad 581–618
Tang	ad 618–907
Five dynasties and ten kingdoms	ad 907–960
Sung (ruled part of China only)	ad 960–1279

Famous Battles of Ancient Times

Marathon Greeks beat Persians
490 bc
Salamis (sea) Greeks beat Persians
480 bc
Gaugamela (Arbela) Greeks beat
Persians 331 bc
Cannae Hannibal beat Romans
216 bc
Actium (sea) Octavian beat Antony
31 bc
Teutoberg Forest Germans beat
Romans 9 bc
Tours (Poitiers) Franks beat
Muslims ad 732

Lechfeld Emperor Otto
beat Magyars ad 955
Hastings Normans
beat English ad 1066
Manzikert Turks beat
Byzantines ad 1071

The Seven Wonders of the Ancient World

The Pyramids of Egypt
Built in the 2000s bc, and the only Wonder to survive. The largest is the Great Pyramid of Cheops, 147 metres high.

Hanging Gardens of Babylon
Terraced gardens built about 600 bc by King Nebuchadnezzar for his wife.

Statue of Zeus at Olympia
Carved by Phidias in the 400s bc. Made of ivory and gold, it stood on the site of the first Olympic Games.

Temple of Artemis at Ephesus
Marble temple with over 100 columns, which took about 120 years to build. Destroyed in ad 262.

Mausoleum at Halicarnassus
Huge tomb in memory of King Mausolus of Caria in Asia Minor, who died in 353 bc.

Colossus of Rhodes
Statue of the sun god Apollo, about 36 metres high, at the harbour entrance. Destroyed by earthquake in 224 bc.

Pharos of Alexandria.
Lighthouse built about 270 bc in harbour of Alexandria, Egypt. Destroyed by earthquake in ad 1375.

Index

A

Abbasid Empire 102
Aborigines 22, 23
Abraham 48
Achaemenid Empire 62
Achilles 71
acropolis 64
actors, Greek 66, 67
Afghanistan 71
Africa
    civilizations 56–7
    first people 20
Agamemnon, mask of 40
agora 64
Ahura Mazda 62, 63
Ainu people 78, 79
Akhenaton 74
Akkad 33, 36
Alexander the Great 44, 63,
    70–1
Alexandria 70, 71
Alfred the Great 110–11, 114
Alfred jewel 111
Americas 58–9, 113
    civilizations 94–5
Amorites 36
Amun, temple of 46
Anasazi people 94
Angles 106
Anglo-Saxon Chronicle 110
antler tools 21, 25
ape-humans 20, 21
Appian Way 83
arch 85
archers 55, 117
Aristarchus 67
Aristotle 67, 70
armour 54, 55
    Greek 65
    Japanese 99

army
    Alexander the Great's 70, 71
    Assyrian 51
    Roman 83, 84, 86, 87, 106
    Persian 63
    see also soldiers
Ashurbanipal 51
Asoka, Emperor 73
Assur 51
Assyria 37, 49, 50, 51, 55
astronomy 37, 97, 103
Athene 67, 88
Athens 64, 65
Augustus 84, 87
Australia
    Aborigines 22, 23
    axes 21, 24, 55
    first people 20

B

Babylon 37, 49, 62, 63
    gates 37
    Ishtar Gate 37
Babylonia 36–7
    classes of people 36
Babylonian Empire 36, 37
Baghdad 103
barbarians 67
barrows 43
Bath 85
bathing/bathrooms
    Mohenjo Daro 39
    Rome 83
Bayeux Tapestry 117
Beaker Folk 43
Belisarius, General 92
Benedictines 105
bezants 93
Bindusara 73

boats
    Ice Age 25
    see also ships
boomerang 23
Boudicca, Queen 87
bread 26, 34
brick-making 35
bricks 31, 35
Britain 106–7, 110–11
    kingdoms 107, 110
British Isles 42, 43
Britons 106
bronze 27
    objects 39, 77, 79
    tools 40, 52, 54, 55
    weapons 52, 54, 55
Bucephalus 70
Buddha 72, 74, 75
Buddhism 74, 75
    in China 76
    in India 72, 73, 74, 75
    in Japan 98
burials
    Japanese 79
    Neanderthal 21
    Yayoi 79
    see also funeral processions
Byzantine Empire 92–3
Byzantium 92

C

Caesar, Julius 84
Cambyses, King 63
Canaan 48, 49
canals 30, 101
caravans, trade 115
Carnac 43
Carolingians 108
Carthage 50, 57

carts 35, 39
castles, Norman 116
cave paintings 23, 25
Celtic
    art and legend 81
    crosses 105
Celts 43, 80–1
Chac Mools 95
Chandragupta Maurya 72
Chang-an 76, 77, 100
chariots
    racing 85, 92
    war 55
Charlemagne 108, 109, 114
Chavin de Huantar 59
Cheops 47
Chichén Itzá 95
chieftains 27, 42
China 52–3, 55, 76–7
    and Japan 78, 79
    cities 115
    culture 101
    dynasties 100–1
    warring states 53
    worship 75
Christendom 115
Christianity 74, 89, 104–5
    eastern orthodox 92, 93
    in Britain 107
cities
    Indus Valley 38, 39
    Maya 95
    Mesopotamia 34
city-states
    Carthage 57
    Near East 32, 33
clay tablets 31, 41
clock
    candle 111
    water 45
Clovis, King 108
Cnut, King 116
coins see money

concrete 85
Confucius 74
Constantine, Emperor 92
Constantinople 92, 93
    Hagia Sophia 93
    Hippodrome 92, 93
consuls 82
copper 27
counting 31
Crete/Cretans 40–1
Cro-Magnons 21
cuneiform writing 31
Cyrus, King 62, 63

D
daily life
    Chinese 52, 76
    Egyptian 45
    Greek 68
    Ice Age 25
    Roman 82, 83, 85
    Viking 112
daimyos 99
Danelaw 111
Danes 110, 111
Darius I, King 62, 65, 73, 71
Dead Sea Scrolls 49
Democritus 66
Diamond Sutra 101
dogs 27
dolmen 43
Dome of the Rock 49, 97
Domesday Book 117
domesticated animals 27, 39
dotaku 79
Dream Time 23
druids 81
Dumnonia 107
dye, purple 51

E
East Anglia 110, 111
Eastern Empire (Roman) 87
Edmund, King 110
Edward the Confessor 116, 117
Egypt 44–7, 48, 70, 71
England 116, 117
English 106
Ethelred, King 116
Etruscans 82, 83
Europe
    Celtic 80-1
    first people 20
    megalithic 40

F
farmers 26–7
    Chavin 59
    Egypt 45
    Greece 67
    Indus Valley 39
    Maya 95
    Sumer 30
Fertile Crescent 27
fire 23
flint tools 21, 24, 25
flying horses 77
forts, Celtic 80
Franks 108–9
Frisians 106
Fujiwaras 98, 99
funeral processions
    Roman 83, 89

G
Gaugamela, battle of 70
Gaul/Gauls 80, 84
Giza 47
gladiators 84
God 48, 49, 75

gods and goddesses
  Babylonian 37
  Celtic 81
  Egyptian 46, 47, 74
  Greek 67, 88, 89
  Hindu 75
  Mesopotamian 31, 32, 35
  Minoan 41
  Persian 63
  Roman 85, 88, 89
  Viking 112, 115
Godwine of Wessex 116
government
  Egyptian 45
  Greek 64
  Roman 86
  Viking 113
grain 26, 31
Great Sphinx 46
Great Pyramids at Giza 47
Great Wall of China 53, 76, 77
Greece 64–9
  art and science 66–7
  vases 69
Greenland 113
gunpowder 101

H
Hadrian, Emperor 87
Hadrian's Wall 87
Hammurabi, King 33, 36, 51
Han dynasty 76–7
Hanno 57
Harappa 38, 39
Harold Hardrada 116, 117
Harold, King 116, 117
Harun al-Rashid 102, 103
Hastings, battle of 117
Heian 98
henges 43
hieroglyphics 45
hillfort 80

Hinduism 72, 74, 75
Hittites 54, 55
Hohokam people 94
Holy Roman Emperor 109
homes see houses
Homo sapiens 20
hoplites 65
horn of Roland 109
houses
  Greece 68
  Indus Valley 38, 39
  Mesopotamia/Sumer 34, 35
  Rome 83
Hsia family 52
Hsiung Nu 77
Huns 77
hunters 21, 22

I
Ice Age 24
Iceland 113
illuminated manuscripts 104, 105
Immortals 63
India 71, 72–3
Indus Valley 38–9
iron 27, 99
Iron Age 27, 43
Islam 96–7, 102
  decoration 97
  symbols 103
Israel 49
Israelites 48, 49
Issus, battle of 70

J
Jainism 75
Japan 78–9, 98–9
  court 98, 99
  provinces 98
Jerusalem 49, 97

Jesus Christ 75
jewellery 31, 113
Jews 48–9, 75
Jorvik (York) 114
Judah 49
Judaism 74, 75
  see also Jews
Judea 49
junks, Chinese 101
Jupiter 88
Justinian, Emperor 92, 93
Jutes 106

K
Kapilavaustu 72
Karnak 46
Khorsabad 51
Kish 32, 33
Knossos, palace of 40, 41
Kush, Kingdom of 56
Kushan 77
Kyoto 98

L
languages
  Arabic 103
  Celtic 80, 81
  Chinese 53
  Latin 85
Latini 82
laws/legal system
  Asoka's 73
  Hammurabi's 33, 36
  Justinian's 92
legate 86
legions 86
lighthouse, Alexandria 71
Liu Pang, Emperor 76
longships 113
Lydia 63

M

MacAlpin, Kenneth 107
Macedonia 70, 71
Magadha, Kingdom of 72
magnetic compass 101
mammoths 24, 25
Marathon, battle of 63, 65
Marduk 37
Martel, Charles 109
Mauryan Empire 71
Maya 95
    ball game 94
Mecca 96, 97
Medes 62
Medina 97
megaliths 42
Menes, King 44
menhirs 43
Mercia 107, 110
Meroë 56
Merovingian dynasty 108
Mesoamerica 58
Mesopotamia 30–5, 36, 51
migrations 22–3
Minoans 40, 41
Minos, King 40, 41
Minotaur 41
Mithra/Mithraism 63
modern humans 20, 21
Mohenjo Daro 38, 39
monasteries 104, 105
money 71, 93, 101
monks 105
Moses 48, 49
Mount Olympus 67, 88
mud brick buildings 31, 35
Muhammad 96, 97
mummies 46, 47
Muslims 97, 115
    empires 102–3
Mycenae 41
    Lion Gate 41
Mycenaeans 40, 41

N

Nabopolassar, General 37
Naram-Sin 33
Naram-Sin Stele 33
Native Americans 94
Neanderthals 20, 21, 22
Near East
    farmers 27
    first people 20
Nebuchadnezzar II 36, 37
Nile River 44, 45
Nineveh 51, 62
Nok people 57
nomads 22
Norman conquest 116–17
Normandy 116
Normans 116, 117
Norsemen 110
North America 113
Northumbria 110
Nubia 56
number system
    Sumer 31
nuns 105

O

Octavian, Augustus 84, 87
Odin 112, 115
Offa of Mercia 107
Olmecs 58, 59
Olympic Games 67, 89
Oracle at Delphi 89
oracle bones 53
ornaments
    Celtic 43, 81
Osiris 46, 47

P

pagans (Britain) 106
paintings, cave 23, 25
paper-making 101

Parthenon 67
Parthia 77
Pataliputra 73
Patna 72, 73
Peloponnesian War 65
Pepin the Short 109
Pericles 64, 65
Persepolis 62, 71
Persia/Persians 62–5, 70
    war with Greece 65
Persian Empire 62–3
    provinces 63
Peru 58
phalanx 65
pharoah 44
Philip of Macedon 70
philosophy 66, 67
Phoenicia/Phoenicians 50, 51,
    57
Pictavia 107
Picts 106
picture-writing 45
Plataea, battle of 65
Porus, King 71
pottery 27, 35, 79, 101
priest kings 39
priest-nobles, Olmec 58
priests
    Babylonia 36
    Celtic 81
    Maya 95
    Mesopotamia 32
provinces, Roman 87
Ptolemy I and II 71
pueblos 94
Punic Wars 50
pyramids 46–7, 58
    step 94, 95

R

Ra 46, 47
Redwald, King 107

reed houses 35
religions, eastern 74–5
Remus 82
roads
    Ice Age 25
    India 73
    Roman 83
rock art 23
Roman
    baths 85
    emperors 86
    gods 88
    Roman Empire 49, 84–7, 92
    Roman Republic 82
    Rome 82, 84–5
    Circus Maximus 85
    towns 85
Romulus 82

S
sacrifices, Maya 95
Sahara 56
Saint Benedict 104
Salamis, battle of 63, 64, 65
samurai 99
Sanchi 72
Sargon of Akkad 33
Sarnath 73
satrap 63
Saxons 106
Scots 106, 107
scribes 31, 33, 45
sculptures
    Assyrian 51
    Nok 57
    Olmec 59
sea trade routes 114
Seleucus Nicator 71
Seljuk Empire 103
Senlac Hill 117
Sennacherib, King 37
shaduf 45

shamans 78, 79
Shang rulers 52, 53
Shih Huang-di 53, 76, 77
Shikibu, Murasaki 99
Shinto 98, 99
ships
    Chinese 101
    Greek 64, 69
    Phoenician 50
    Viking 110, 112, 113
Shotoku, Prince 98
silk 77
Silk Road 77, 115
slaves 65, 85
Socrates 67
soldiers 54, 55
    Chinese 77
    Greek 65
    Japanese 99
    Persian 63
    Roman 84, 86
    see also army
Solomon, King 49
Sparta 64, 65
Sphinx, Great 46
Stamford Bridge, battle of
    117
stone
    heads 59
    monuments 42–3, 47
Stone Age 21
Stonehenge 43
stupa 72
Sui emperors 100
Sumer 30, 35, 36
Sung dynasty 100, 101
Sutton Hoo 107
Sweyn Forkbeard, King 116

T
Tang dynasty 100
Temple of Jerusalem 49

temples
    Egyptian 46
    Greek and Roman 89
    Mesopotamian 32, 35
    Olmec 58
    Teotihuacán 94
Ten Commandments 48, 49
Teotihuacán 94
terracotta army 77
The Tale of Genji 99
The Thousand and One Nights
    102
theatre, Greek 66, 67
Thebes 70
Theodora, Empress 92, 93
Thermopylae, battle of 65
things 113
Tiahuanaco 94
tool-making 24
tools
    Cretan 40
    farming 26
    Ice Age 24, 25
    metal 27
    Stone Age 20, 21
torii 99
trade
    Abbasid 103
    China 76, 77
    Crete 40
    Greece 69
    Indus Valley 39
    Viking 112
trade routes 114–15
    African 56
    Ice Age 25
Trajan, Emperor 87
Tutankhamun 47

U
Ummayid family 102
Ur 33, 36, 48
    standard of 33

Uruk 32, 33
   White Temple 35

V
Valley of the Kings 47
Vikings 110, 111, 112–13, 114,
   116
villages
   Iron Age 27
   European 42, 43
villas, Roman 83, 85

W
war see soldiers, weapons
weapons 54–5
   Frankish 109
   Japanese 99
   metal 27
   Persian 63
Wessex 107, 110
Westminster Abbey 116, 117
wheat 26
wheel 27, 35
wheelbarrow 100, 101
William Duke of Normandy
   (King William I) 116, 117
wolf cubs 26
women
   Greece 69
   Mesopotamia 32
   shamans 78
writing
   Babylonian 37
   Chinese 53
   Cretan and Mycenaean 41
   Egyptian 45
   Greek 65
   Japanese 99
   Sumerian 31
Wu-ti, Emperor 77

X
Xerxes 63

Y
Yamato clan 79
Yayoi 78, 79

Z
Zarathustra (Zoroaster) 63
Zeus 67, 88, 89
Zhou 52
ziggurats 34, 35